NKF: PIET ZWART'S
AVANT-GARDE CATALOG
FOR STANDARD CABLES,
1927–1928

NKF:
PIET
ZWART'S
AVANT-
GARDE
CATALOG

FOR STANDARD CABLES, 1927–1928'

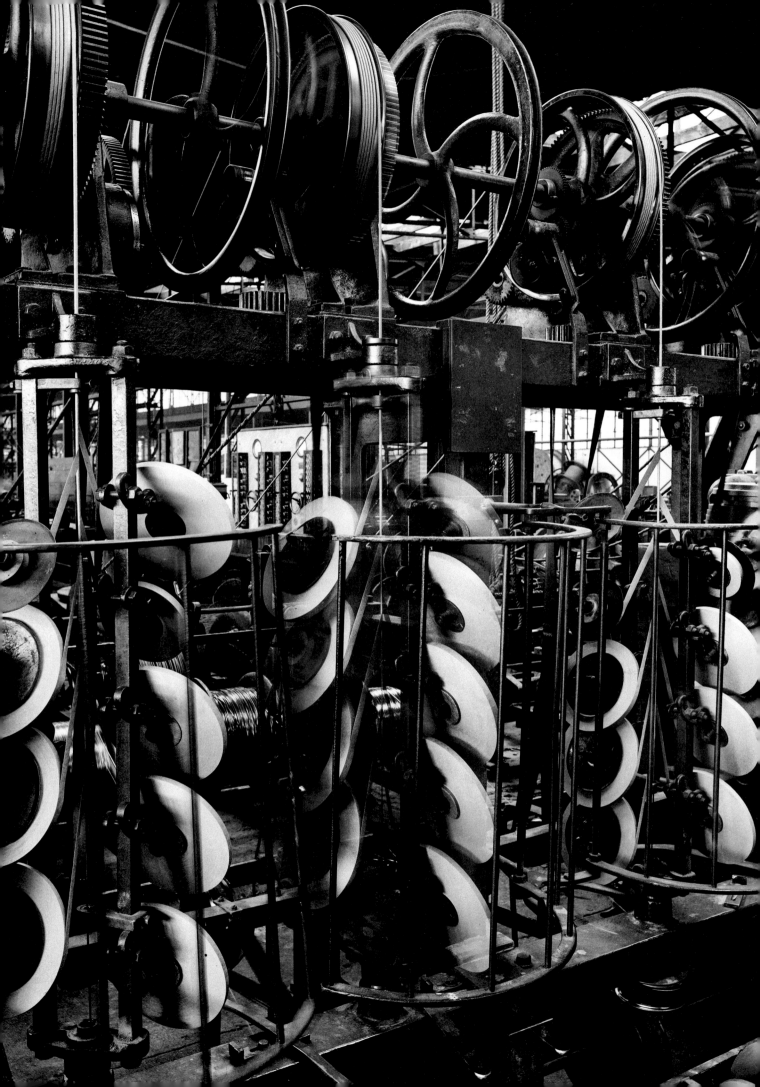

PHILIP B. MEGGS

PIET ZWART'S NKF CATALOG

7

Writing to a friend in 1926 about his current activities, designer Piet Zwart said, "I also have much advertising work. I do this for relaxation. I have achieved quite something in this, especially for the Nederlandsche Kabelfabriek [NKF, Netherlands Cable Works] in Delft. Although these designs appear to be very simple things without much pretension, I find this work very important as a sign of our times. . . . It relates to my total perception of the mind and the tasks of this time period. It is a very multisided work. I am now working on a foreign catalog for the NKF in which I am creating some very strange things."[1]

In a letter to his wife, Nel, Zwart added, "There will be some significant things in [the catalog], and I am trying various experiments which, I think, have never been used in advertising."[2]

Zwart was part of an international movement after World War I to "give a new form to typography. The common goal of every endeavor was not so much to improve typography as to reform a branch of art that had lost all distinction. An endlessly swelling flood of printed matter, a gray boundless sea of uniformity, was crying out for some kind of revolution."[3]

Innovation and experimentation often seem raw and extreme when they first appear; only later, after the forms and spatial arrangements have filtered into the mainstream of mass communications, are they accepted and incorporated into the design vocabulary. Today, the NKF catalog appears as functional–even classic–modernism, but in the 1920s, it was a radical application of a new design vocabulary to a large industrial firm's publicity material. The NKF management was willing to risk the use of designs not yet proven in the realm of business competition. This evinces a rare managerial trait: a capacity to lead rather than follow.

This eighty-page, perfect-bound volume was issued in 1928. Red, yellow, blue, and black inks were printed by letterpress on a glossy white coated stock. The European DIN A4 format was used, with pages approximately 11½ by 8¼ inches (29.5 by 21 cm). In addition to the Dutch-language version, an English-language edition was published.

Traditional hierarchy and structure of page layout were rejected by Zwart, whose asymmetrical page layouts are vigorous and open. He created a cinematic visual flow from spread to spread; elements echo earlier elements, and the placement of the focal point in the spreads keeps changing unexpectedly.

Razor-sharp photographs of cables and cable cross-sections move in syncopated rhythms with diagonal bars and lines of text. Zwart often wrote his own copy, so form and message are merged into a dynamic unity. White space becomes an important design element, ebbing and flowing as photographs and type expand and contract through the book.

The NKF catalog was innovative in its form and space, but this inventiveness was designed to effectively present factual catalog information through lucid words and images. Zwart's modernism was not about style or visual effects; rather, it was about innovating ways to engage the reader and effectively communicate messages.

The cover **1** displays the NKF initials and logo–a circular cross-section of a three-strand cable printed on yellow cover-weight paper. The opening spread **2** provides Zwart's first visual jolt. A large black logo thrusts downward on the yellow left-hand page, while the initials NKF are printed in overlapping red and blue at the top of the right-hand page. A vertical black bar bleeds down from the top on the left-hand page, and another bleeds up from the bottom on the right-hand page. These bars become a structural theme throughout the book. Zwart

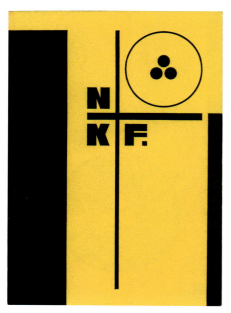

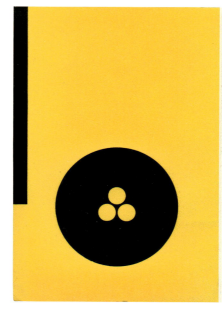

N.V. NEDERLANDSCHE KABELFABRIEK DELFT

1

8

creates two imaginary horizontal lines moving across the space and aligning with the ends of these bars, and a third one runs between these two. Elements are aligned with these three positions on many spreads, creating a visual flow. Page numbers are consistently placed at the ends of the bars. Zwart said the black bars protect the paper from being marred when the book is handled.

The next spread **3** reverses the movement. The left-hand circle becomes yellow and rises upward, while overprinted blue and red slabs on the lower right present an aerial photograph of the factory. The area of the blue halftone overprinted by red becomes purple, thereby separating the NKF factory from the other buildings in the photograph. These have a dynamic downward thrust, balanced by the upward thrust of the company name.

The content is presented in three sections. The opening section is eight pages long and introduces the reader to NKF through interior and exterior photographs of the factory, accompanied by a descriptive statement about the company and its philosophy. As the reader turns to pages 4 and 5 **4**, the catalog goes from the exterior to the massive interior of the factory. Pages 10 and 11 **5** have a caption on the left: "From wirebar to wire in our rolling works. We supply wire in other profiles besides round." Diagrams at the bottom of page 10 identify round, flat, and square wire configurations. The title on the right-hand page identifies the section of the wire drawing plant where brass wire is worked. The yellow circle from page 2 reappears, relating back to the earlier page. Zwart delighted in repeating forms with size and color changes.

Photography was becoming increasingly important in Zwart's work during this period. He retained a photographer to make the close-up photographs of cutaway cable specimens and cross sections. He also began to make photographs and photograms

9

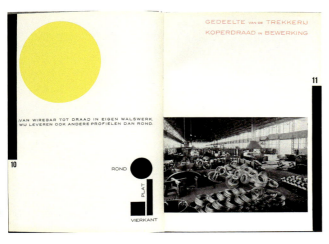

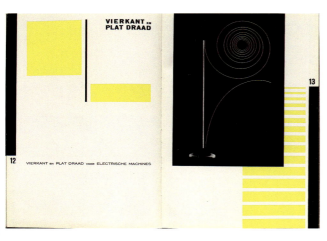

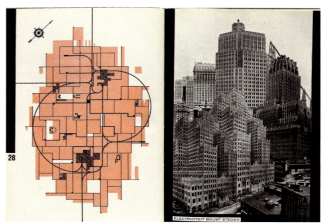

himself. Pages 12 and 13 **6** display "square and flat wires for electrical machines." In this superb page composition, every form makes a statement. The yellow square and rectangle on the left signify square and flat wires, respectively; the sequence of yellow rectangles on the right symbolizes the variety of sizes; and the photogram of wires demonstrates their flexibility. The relationship between the two vertical lines creates unity. Zwart learned relational composition from painters, especially artists of the Dutch De Stijl movement. Pages 18 and 19 **7** have six paper swatches tipped in on a ruled grid structure that becomes part of the composition.

An innovative layout appears on pages 26 and 27. **8** The left-hand page has a montage relating to the generation, transmission, and use of electrical power. A red arrow zooms from a caption,

"The secure foundation for modern industry," to a cross-section of an NKF cable. The dynamic typography on the right translates, "DECISION! / BREAKDOWN // how much would a BREAKDOWN set you back? // use an 'NKF CABLE' and forget / the word BREAKDOWN."

Pages 28 and 29 **9** present two views of the electrified modern city: a diagrammatic map and a photomontage of high-rise buildings.

In the book's large central section, NKF's product line of electrical and telephone cables is illustrated and described. Descriptive data and photography combine to give viewers an immediate understanding of the various cables. Silhouetted cable photographs are arrowlike shapes slashing across the page. Diagonal cable photographs are composed against horizontal and vertical typography and rules on some spreads; other spreads have vertical photographs in spatial opposition to diagonal type. Cross-section and profile photographs provide immediate understanding of the structure of each wire.

The page designs make information instantly accessible. Pages 30 and 31 [10] present single-core 600-volt cable manufactured to Dutch regulations N 217: Three versions are clearly identified as: 1) with solid conductor; 2) with stranded conductor; and 3) with stranded conductor and pilot wire. The note on the right-hand page translates to "⅔ actual size." One spread after the next [11], Zwart places type and images on the diagonal. The copy reads, "Multicore/500-volt/light construction/Dutch regulations/N 219." The captions identify two-, three-, and four-core cables.

Zwart introduces new forms [12], such as the blue square containing a photograph of a "six-core high-current cable for 10,000 volts/applied for the split

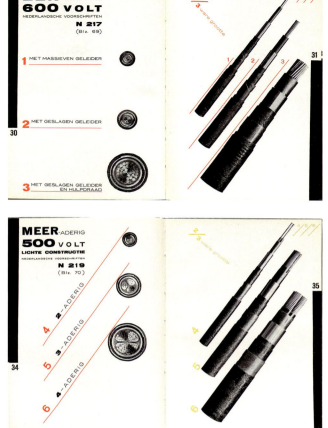

21

HOOGSPANNINGSKABEL MET GEPATENTEERDE METAALLAGEN

GEMETALLISEERD PAPIER OM DE ADERS

"H" KABEL

"H"

21
"H"

46

47

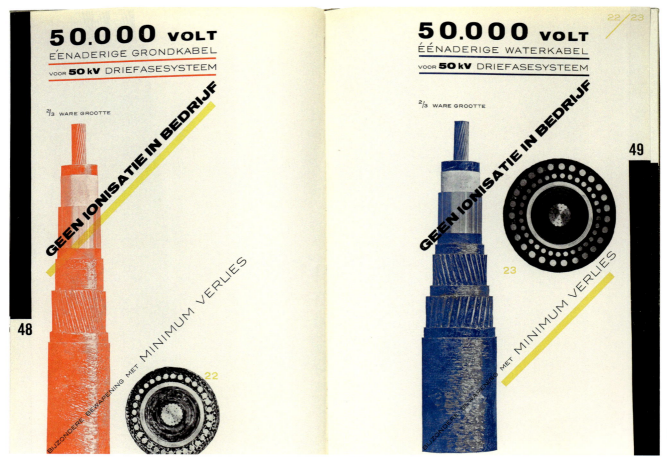

50.000 VOLT
ÉÉNADERIGE GRONDKABEL
VOOR **50 kV** DRIEFASESYSTEEM

²/₃ WARE GROOTTE

GEEN IONISATIE IN BEDRIJF

BIJZONDERE BEWAPENING MET MINIMUM VERLIES

48

22

50.000 VOLT
ÉÉNADERIGE WATERKABEL
VOOR **50 kV** DRIEFASESYSTEEM

²/₃ WARE GROOTTE

GEEN IONISATIE IN BEDRIJF

BIJZONDERE BEWAPENING MET MINIMUM VERLIES

22/23

49

23

conductor safety system." Bold type overprinting the image proclaims, "Split conductor of the future." On the opposite page, a black-and-white photograph of a "three-core high-tension cable for 30,000 volts/with belt insulation zone" overprints the yellow circle seen on earlier spreads.

Pages 46 and 47 **13** feature a high-tension cable with patented metallic sheathing around the cores. The cross section of this three-segment cable inspired the NKF trademark.

Faced with page after page of cable photographs and product information, Zwart innovated page-design variations. Pages 48 and 49 **14** depict 50,000-volt single-core underground (left) and submarine (right) cables with a 50-kilovolt three-phase system and special armoring for minimal loss. Pages 48 and 49 are almost identical, but the left halftone is printed in red, the right one in blue. Black type and a yellow bar overprint the photographs. Zwart establishes repetition, then breaks it by shifting the position of the yellow bars and cross-section photographs.

On pages 50 and 51 **15**, Zwart shows his brilliance at taking simple type matter and using size, weight, color, and position to enliven the ordinary. An advertising slogan on page 50 loosely translates, "WE don't want a 'satisfied' consumer / WE want an 'enthusiastic' consumer." Page 51 opens the section showing telephone cables.

This section makes extensive use of enlarged detail photographs to show the cable construction. On pages 56 and 57 **16**, the left photograph is identified as 30-segment telephone cable; the detail at right has a caption: "Each core is surrounded by an aluminum coil." Red dots are used to signify the relative scale of the two images. On pages 60 and 61 **17**, a different device, a red dot overprinting a blue halftone, is used to identify the segment enlarged as a circular photograph. The left caption

15

16

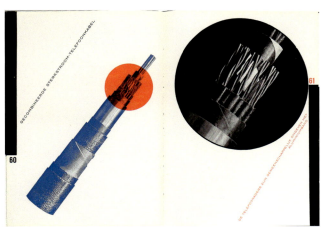

17

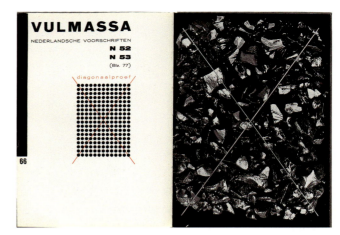

identifies a combination power and telephone cable; the right states that the telephone cores are collectively surrounded by aluminum tape.

The opening spread **18** for the section on signaling and block cables opens with a photomontage showing a control panel and filmstrips of a railroad switch and locomotive. A lively rhythm of diagonals is punctuated by the blue silhouetted control panel moving back in space on the left.

A miscellaneous product, filling mass used for insulation, is presented on pages 66 and 67 **19** through a full-page photograph and a smaller diagram. Page 68 **20** illustrates a telephone cable with a high–self-induction system. This is the final illustrated page; page 69 opens a ten-page section of technical specifications and engineering data.

An ordinary, even pedestrian, line of industrial products is presented in a book that has been hailed as a breakthrough achievement in early twentieth-century graphic design. The designer's vision transcended subject matter, even as it focused on the applied design problem of presenting this subject matter to readers. Zwart's background, philosophy, and influences clarify how and why this happened.

Zwart began his career as an interior and furniture designer and arrived at graphic design by a circuitous route. He was born on May 28, 1885, in Zaandijk, Holland, and educated at Amsterdam's National School of Applied Arts from 1902 to 1907. While there, Zwart embraced strong beliefs including humanitarian, pacifist, theosophical, and socialist doctrines. He became a vegetarian and adopted a philosophy espousing a simple approach to life.

From 1908 until 1913, Zwart taught art history and drawing courses at the Technical and Domestic Science School for Girls in Leeuwarden. During this period, he produced interior, fabric, and furniture designs.

Decorative and floral motifs characterize much of Zwart's work before 1919, when he first had contact with De Stijl—the Dutch movement founded in 1917 by Piet Mondrian, Theo van Doesburg, and others. Although Zwart was deeply influenced by De Stijl's reduction of art and design to elemental geometric structures and pure primary colors, he never became a member of the group.

From 1919 to 1921, Zwart worked in the office of architect Jan Wils, who belonged to De Stijl from the very beginning, and collaborated on furniture designs with De Stijl member Vilmos Huszár. For Zwart, De Stijl's strict vocabulary of horizontals and verticals and primary colors was too limiting; he was unwilling to banish other elements, such as churning diagonal thrusts and the color green, from his work.

Shortly before joining H. P. Berlage's architectural office in The Hague in 1921, Zwart executed his first typographic designs: stationery for architect Jan Wils and printed matter for Vickers House, a manufacturer of flooring. In his earliest works, after making a rough sketch, Zwart ordered proofs of type, rules, and symbols from the printers. At his drafting table, these typographic materials became collage elements, which Zwart moved around as he searched for a dynamic and functional spatial arrangement. He approached page layout as a searching process and kept an open mind, unfettered by preconceived notions or typographic conventions.

The following year, Zwart met the Russian constructivist El Lissitzky and found that they were exploring similar typographic designs. This encounter reinforced Zwart's direction, as did his meetings with the German collagist Kurt Schwitters. The Dada movement was an important resource, for its emphasis upon chance, process, and a playful manipulation of elements inspired Zwart's keen sense of experimentation.

About design's social role, Zwart said, "Design is not a matter of taste but an expression of our attitude toward life, dictated by the meta cosmos. Design and use of material are not matters of individual whim, but responsible factors in the community."[4] A profound concern for the reader characterized Zwart's graphic designs. He believed the fast pace of twentieth-century life robbed people of adequate time to read and absorb vast amounts of gray text. Innovative ways to present messages were clearly needed. White space, diagonal movements, and contrast of scale and weight were used to engage readers and propel them forward into the material. Static symmetrical balance was rejected; space was made active and fused into a dynamic whole. Copy was stripped to its essence.

In 1923, Berlage introduced the 37-year-old Zwart to one of his relatives, who was a director of the NKF in Delft. Soon Zwart was designing their publicity, and graphic design began to consume much of his time. The ads, brochures, and catalogs he designed for NKF number in the hundreds [see pages 50–71 of the present volume]. Zwart became active as a photographer in 1926, and this influenced his graphic design.

While the NKF catalog is widely regarded as Zwart's masterpiece, his work continued unabated after this remarkable accomplishment. In 1930, he began a twelve-year association with PTT, the Netherlands postal, telephone, and telegraph agency. Commissions from PTT included the design of postage stamps and postal indicias, advertising and publicity, and exhibitions. The Bruynzeel firm, a manufacturer of wood products, was an important client for whom Zwart designed new product lines, notably modular kitchen components in 1937. This project had a tremendous impact on kitchen design.

In 1943 and 1944, Zwart was under Nazi detention and kept apart from his wife and four children. After the war, he resumed his collaboration with Bruynzeel and produced new stamps for the PTT.

Zwart died in Leidschendam on September 24, 1977, at age 92. His legacy is a profound influence on graphic design that spans the globe.

In 1937, Zwart explained his approach to typographic design: "The task of functional typography is to create a form of typographical design in harmony with the present age, a form free of traditional conventions and as animated as possible; it is to find a clear, well-ordered means of visual expression that shall be decided by modern typographical problems and modern methods (e.g., phototype, techniques such as machine setting, typewriter script, and photographic setting); it is to break with the spirit of handwork."[5] His designs for NKF, including the catalog, achieved a remarkable functional vitality and are a historically important expression of a dynamic age of change. About the NKF catalog, Zwart said, "What is the beauty of this kind of work? That it is a slice of life, and that it also is your whole life?"[6] Seldom has the viewpoint of designer as artist been so eloquently expressed.

Endnotes

1 Piet Zwart, quoted in Kees Broos, *Piet Zwart* (The Hague: Haags Gemeentemuseum, 1973), 46.

2 Piet Zwart, quoted in Arthur A. Cohen, *Herbert Bayer and Piet Zwart: Masters of Design* (New York: Ex Libris, undated), 14.

3 Hans L. C. Jaffé, "Piet Zwart: A Pioneer of Functional Typography," *Neue Grafik* 10 (1961): 6.

4 Piet Zwart, *Keywords/Sleutelwoorden* (The Hague: Staatsdrukkerij Den Haag, 1966), 6.

5 Zwart, quoted in Jaffé, 9.

6 Zwart, quoted in Broos, 46.

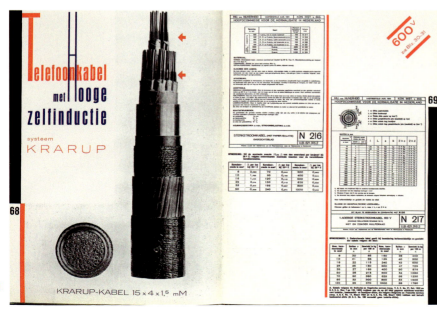

PAUL STIRTON

PIET ZWART, NKF, AND THE NEW TYPOGRAPHY

17

In the spring of 1923, Piet Zwart was introduced to C. F. Proos (1886–1973), technical director of the cable manufacturer Nederlandse Kabelfabriek (NKF, Netherlands Cable Works), the industrial firm that would become Zwart's principal graphic design client. Zwart was thirty-seven at the time and well established as an assistant in the office of H. P. Berlage (1856–1934), the presiding master of progressive architecture in the Netherlands. Proos was Berlage's son-in-law, married to the architect's eldest daughter, Cornelia ("Corrie"), and in search of someone to create promotional materials for his company. Although trained as a metallurgist, Proos was by no means insensitive to the arts, as suggested by his bookplate, commissioned from the left-leaning printmaker, Johan van Hell, which includes a line from Walt Whitman's poem "Crossing Brooklyn Ferry." **1** Arranging for Zwart to produce a series of advertisements for NKF in specialist trade journals, Proos sparked a burst of intense innovation in the emerging designer's practice.

NKF was still a relatively new company, set up in 1913 by Cornelis von Lindern (1869–1945), the eldest son of an entrepreneurial family from Alblasserdam in the southern Netherlands with interests in ship-building and rope making. **2** Although von Lindern had little or no experience in metalworking, he recognized the potential of adapting the principles of rope making to the expanding industry of electrical cable manufacturing. It was an opportune moment. NKF underwent a dramatic expansion during the First World War due to the increased demand for its products and a corresponding decline in German imports. By the early 1920s,

it had become a substantial industrial concern, although it was still a young company without a distinct commercial identity. Over the next decade, Zwart would produce over 275 designs for advertisements, as well as catalogs, stationery, and exhibition displays for NKF, establishing a reputation for himself and crafting the image of a company at the forefront of a technological age. In essence, Zwart transformed the humble yet quintessentially modern cable into a subject for experimental graphic design. In doing so, he made NKF the patron and vehicle of one of the most outstanding contributions to the international avant-garde.

The NKF advertisements were not Zwart's first foray into experimental design work. His training as an architect between 1902 and 1907 at the National School of Applied Arts (Rijksschool voor Kunstnijverheid) in Amsterdam was broad ranging and apparently quite unstructured. **3** As Zwart himself

1

2

recalled, "There were times when we didn't see a teacher in weeks," thus allowing the adventurous student to explore many areas of craft and design without observing any rigid disciplinary boundaries.[1] After college, with no clear plans or career ahead, Zwart took on various temporary jobs, teaching in schools and colleges, until in 1919, following military service, he joined the recently established office of the architect Jan Wils (1891–1972). Wils had briefly been associated with De Stijl, the most severe and uncompromising of all the avant-garde groups in Europe. Founded in Leiden in 1917 by Theo van Doesburg (1883–1931) and Piet Mondrian (1872–1944), De Stijl advocated pure abstraction and the strict adherence to the most basic visual elements: primary colors and rectilinear forms in both art and architecture. Although Wils had moved away from the more rigid constraints of De Stijl, Zwart recalled that he "worked in the spirit of De Stijl"

and engaged with others connected to the movement.[2] As a member of the Hague Art Circle (Haagse Kunstkring), Wils introduced Zwart to a wide community of progressive artists and ideas, not least in the person of the Hungarian artist Vilmos Huszár (1884–1960), also a former member of De Stijl and the designer of their magazine's first cover. 4 During the 1920s, Huszár expanded his interests to embrace advertising and furniture design, collaborating with Zwart on interior design projects while maintaining his contacts with many of the leading figures of the European avant-garde.

The aesthetic values of the Hague Art Circle were bound up with ideas of the rebirth of society on modern, egalitarian lines, in accordance with a broader upsurge in utopian thinking and an impulse for reform following the First World War. Many artists and designers felt that they were on the threshold of revolutionary change and that notions of

19

3

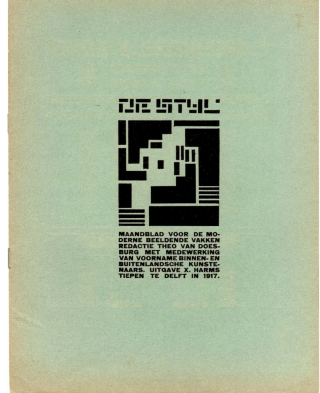

4

1 Johan van Hell, bookplate for C. F. Proos, 1925, wood engraving, 2¾ × 2 inches (7 × 5 cm), Amsterdam.
2 Directors and management of the Nederlandse Kabelfabriek (NKF, Netherlands Cable Works), 1938. At the center of the photograph are Cornelis von Lindern (left) and C. F. Proos (right). Behind them, a tapestry from the studio of J. F. Semey commemorates the twenty-fifth anniversary of the company.
3 Students at the National School of Applied Arts (Rijksschool voor Kunstnijverheid) in Amsterdam, circa 1906. Piet Zwart stands in the middle row at the far right.
4 Vilmos Huszár, cover design for *De Stijl*, 1917, offset lithography, 8⅞ × 5⅞ inches (22.5 × 15 cm), Leiden.

beauty, taste, and modernity had to be linked with a universalist impulse to remake society. In a 1919 lecture to the group, Zwart himself observed, "Our time has become characterized by an enthusiastic desire for change, born out of a growing discontent over social conditions, determined and guided by new means of production, new spiritual insights, and new ideals."[3] An early indication of Zwart's radical politics and his willingness to engage in public debate on matters he felt strongly about, his statement also presages a period of restless innovation in his design work.

The link to De Stijl, albeit secondhand, is evident in Zwart's earliest graphic works. Although primarily engaged with furniture and interior design during his time with Wils, Zwart was tasked with designing the office's stationery as a way of expressing its architectural ideals. Employing sans serif lettering and assemblages of rectangular blocks, Zwart's headed notepaper and postcards recall the forms and ideals found in the *De Stijl* journal edited by Van Doesburg. **5** This was the kind of design, combining text, letterforms, and the graphic equivalents of basic building materials, that would eventually lead Zwart to describe his hybrid role as that of a *typotekt*: a fusion of typographer and architect.[4]

In the early 1920s, Zwart produced promotional designs for a few other organizations, including the Verloop housing office and the vegetarian restaurant and hotel Pomona. His work for the latter reveals a playful, experimental approach inspired by the irreverent and unruly Dada art movement as exemplified in printed matter by Van Doesburg and German artist Kurt Schwitters (1887–1948). **6** The finest examples of this early phase in his career, however, are to be found in the advertisements Zwart produced in 1922 and 1923 for the British firm Vickers House, which imported construction tools, materials, and flooring. Zwart's postcard

advertisements in particular demonstrate the complex effects he could achieve when working on a small scale, using only the resources of the letterpress printshop. In a card advertising saws, drills, and files ("zagen, boren, vijlen"), he deploys printer's rules or space bars locked together as printing elements to create lines and a green square around which various blocks of text and geometric shapes are arranged.[5] **7** Zwart plays with the letterforms not only as abstract elements in the design, but also as vehicles for visual puns and variations on meaning. Note how each of the words for tools points to that tool's essential shape in the left-hand column—the triangular teeth of the saw, the diminishing circular drill holes, the rasp of the files indicated by small lozenge shapes—while ending in the right-hand column in a single elongated *N* that concludes all three words. Zwart further animates the design by directing our eye downward from the steep crossbar of this letter to the smaller black *N* letterforms before ending in an uppercase *H*. A witty exercise in semiotics, the advertisement's forms, words, and meanings make up an abstract diagram that invites us to identify signifying relationships while leading our eye around the pictorial field. But Zwart is also testing the materials of the printer's case to their limits to produce the most concentrated visual effects. As he would later write in a letter to his wife, "Typography is the printing method in which you can only use the material that the printer has; so you have to compose with a fixed and limited number of resources. I believe that there is not a hint of pedantry in this."[6]

The choreography of the eye in this example indicates how Zwart sought to introduce a sense of movement into what is essentially a static design. Many commentators have pointed out how the repeated triangular barbs of the saw and descending *N* letterforms evoke the flow of film stock through a

5

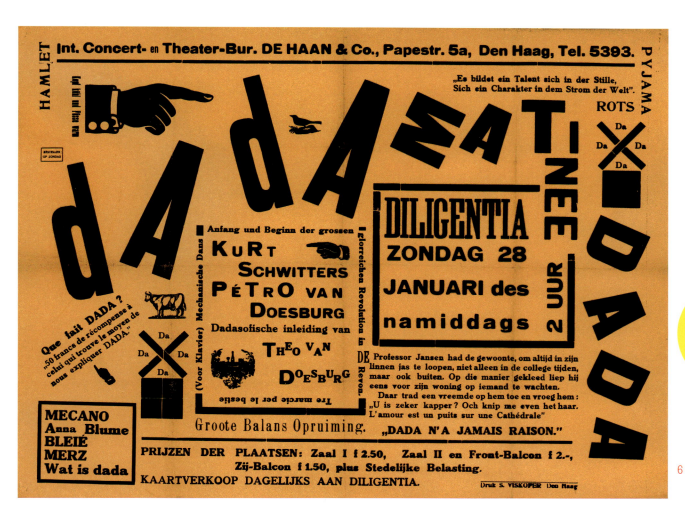

HET LINNEN VENSTER

DOOR
C.J. GRAADT VAN ROGGEN

INLEIDING TOT DE
SERIE MONOGRAFIEËN OVER
FILMKUNST ONDER REDACTIE
VAN Mr C.J. GRAADT VAN ROGGEN

W.L. & J. BRUSSE N.V. ROTTERDAM

N° 1

8 Piet Zwart, cover design for *The Linen
Window* (*Het linnen venster*), the first
volume in the series Monographs on
the Art of Film (Monografieën over
filmkunst), 1931, offset lithography,
8⅝ × 6⅞ inches (22 × 17.5 cm), Rotterdam.

projector, while the shapes and words seem set to move in an animated sequence.[7] An avid cinema-goer with strong views on film as a creative medium, Zwart looked to the movies for keys to unlock the dynamic potential of static images.[8] Later in his career, in 1928, he would design a famous poster for an experimental film festival in The Hague (Internationale Tentoonstelling Op Filmgebied), and three years later he designed the photomontage covers for a series of books on current trends in international film. In each case, the conception expresses some aspect of the technology of projecting film or of the experience of watching a movie. **8**

One of the prompts for this new phase of Zwart's work was his meeting with the Soviet architect-designer El Lissitzky (1890–1941). Residing in Germany for part of the 1920s, Lissitzky acted as a sort of emissary for the Soviet avant-garde, organizing exhibitions, publishing articles, and producing his own journal, *Vehsch/Gegenstand/Objet* ("object" in Russian, German, and French, respectively), with the writer Ilya Ehrenburg. Lissitzky was also personally active in networking among groups of avant-garde artists and designers in Central and Western Europe, giving talks and corresponding with an expanding circle of friends and collaborators. Zwart attended a lecture El Lissitzky gave for the Hague Art Circle on May 18, 1923, and was introduced to the Russian by Huszár, Lissitzky's host during his visit. Lissitzky showed Zwart some of his recent graphics and presented him with a copy of *About Two Squares* (*Pro dva kvadrata*).[9] **9** This groundbreaking work, ostensibly a children's book, recounts the exploits of a red square and a black square that descend to Earth, where the red square establishes a new world order. On one level, the book is a piece of Bolshevik propaganda. At the same time, *About Two Squares* is explicitly an exercise in sequential abstract composition, an implied narrative or animation of formal motifs with roots in Suprematism, the Russian art movement that employed basic geometric forms to suggest a higher plane of artistic feeling. But beyond its content, the book also demonstrates the power of print to communicate ideas graphically, employing basic formal and textual elements in ways Zwart would further explore while securing his professional identity through his typographic work for NKF. **10**

This formative encounter took place at a momentous time for the developing new aesthetics of rationalism, abstraction, and technology. Contemporary culture in Central Europe was still dominated by expressionism; its emphasis on a subjective view of the world, often distorted to heighten emotional impact, perhaps found its best outlet in film and drama. The new aesthetics, however, favored a more detached and orderly approach that was especially effective in the field

23

9

9   El Lissitzky, *About Two Squares: A Suprematist Tale of Two Squares in Six Constructions* (*Pro dva kvadrata. Suprematicheskii skaz v 6-ti postroikakh*), 1922, letterpress, 8½ × 10½ inches (21.5 × 26.75 cm), Berlin.

10 Piet Zwart, business card with artist's monogram, undated, letterpress, 2 × 3⅛ inches (5 × 8 cm), Wassenaar.

10

11

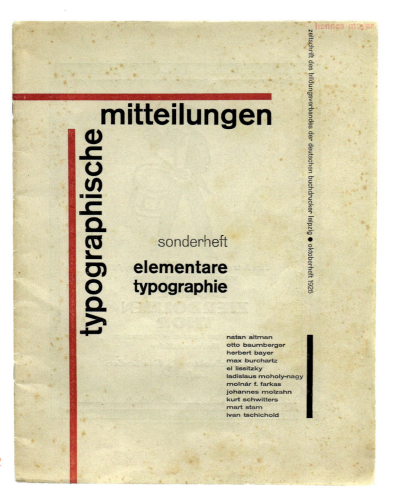

12

11 Participants of the International
Congress of Constructivists and
Dadaists on the steps of the Thuringia
State Museum in Weimar, 1922. László
Moholy-Nagy stands at the far right of
the top row. El Lissitzky holds a pipe
in his mouth in the next row from the
top. In the middle row, Max Burchartz
carries a child on his shoulders, and
Theo van Doesburg wears the cover
of *De Stijl* on his hat. In the next row
down, Tristan Tzara presses his cheek
against Nelly van Moorsel's (later van
Doesburg) hand. Sophie Taeuber-Arp
and Hans Arp stand to the right of
him, and Hans Richter reclines on
the ground in front.

12 Jan Tschichold, cover of *Typographic
Notes, Special Issue: Fundamental
Typography* (*Typographische Mitteilungen, Sonderheft: Elementare Typographie*), October 1925, letterpress,
12¼ × 9¼ inches (31 × 23.5 cm), Leipzig.

of print, where systematic organization of elements came to the fore. The shift was not merely a matter of clarity. Between 1923 and 1925, a fundamentally new concept of typographic design emerged in connection with some of the most radical and utopian ideas about art, society, and mass communication. The early stirrings could be observed at the rather grandly titled International Congress of Constructivists and Dadaists organized by Van Doesburg in Weimar in September 1922.[10] [11] This meeting drew an odd assortment of modern artists, including Hans Arp, Hans Richter, Sophie Taeuber-Arp, and Tristan Tzara from Zurich's Dada movement, alongside a number of more practically engaged artist-designers. Among the latter group, Lissitzky, Schwitters, László Moholy-Nagy (1895–1946), Max Burchartz (1887–1961), and Werner Graeff (1901–78) would each make important contributions to what became known as the New Typography. Although absent from the Congress, Zwart came to know most of these figures personally, and he became especially close to Schwitters, whom he met through Huszár the following year.

The term New Typography first appeared as the title of a short essay by Moholy-Nagy in the catalog for the landmark 1923 exhibition at the Bauhaus, Germany's pioneering architecture and design school, but what began as a manifesto would quickly grow into a broad international movement that aimed to revolutionize how printed matter was designed.[11] Like other radical art and architecture movements of the time, it came armed with its own body of theory, initially voiced in a blizzard of polemical statements about typography and its role in the formation of a modern sensibility. El Lissitzky led the way with his article "Topography of Typography," in the Dada journal *Merz*, in July 1923. The next year Schwitters responded

with "Theses on Typography," also in *Merz*, and Burchartz produced his manifesto, "Advertising Design." In 1925 El Lissitzky returned to the subject in an article entitled "Typographical Facts," while Moholy-Nagy proposed the concept of "typophoto" in his book *Painting, Photography, Film*, all of which were followed by statements from other artist-designers such as Willi Baumeister (1889–1955), Walter Dexel (1890–1973), and Johannes Molzahn (1892–1965).[12] These manifestos and polemics had several points in common. Their ideas were often delivered in the form of rules or commandments reflecting the high stakes that the new generation placed upon the medium of graphic communication.

The groundswell of disparate voices and activities across many cities was brought into focus by Jan Tschichold (1902–74), a young German designer trained as a typographer and calligrapher but, like Zwart, excited by the possibilities suggested in these new theories of design and communication. In 1924 he began gathering material for a special issue of *Typographic Notes* (*Typographische Mitteilungen*), the journal of the educational wing of the Union of German Book Printers (Bildungsverband der Deutschen Buchdrucker), which enjoyed a wide readership in the trade. The issue eventually appeared in October 1925 under the title "elementare typographie" ("elemental" or "fundamental typography"), all lowercase, with an asymmetrical layout and bold rectilinear block lines in red and black.[13] [12] The publication was a startling expression of the new ideas in both its form and content. Tschichold prominently featured work by El Lissitzky, and went so far as to adopt the Russian version of his own name: Iwan (or Ivan, as it appears on the cover). He also contributed his ten commandments to the growing body of texts, repeating many of the points already made. These could be paraphrased in a few simple statements:

— typography has a purpose, so it must express the message clearly and simply;
— the central division of the page should be abandoned in favor of asymmetrical layout;
— the elemental letterform is the sans serif, and we must consider using only lowercase type;
— vertical and diagonal lines, different shapes, and multiple font sizes may be used simultaneously to increase the urgency of the message;
— elemental design excludes the use of any ornament; and
— in today's optical world, the exact image is created by photography.

25

cht zusammenstimmen könnten. Beide zusammen ergeben
leichmäßiges Grau, denn ihre Harmonie beruht gerade auf
nd Farbkontrast. Beiden ist aber gemeinsam: die Objektivität
iche Form, die sie als zeitgemäße Mittel erweist. Die Harmonie
bloß eine äußerlich formale, wie sie früher irrtümlich ange-
war, und auch keine Willkürlichkeit; denn es gibt nur eine
iftform — die Grotesk — und nur eine objektive Aufzeichnung
elt — die Photographie.
individualistischen Form der Graphik: Handschrift — Zeichnung
ektive Form: Typo — Photo gegenübergetreten.
bezeichnen wir jede Synthese von Typographie und Photo-
e können wir mit Hilfe des Photos vieles besser und schneller
s auf den umständlichen Wegen der Rede oder Schreibe. Das
reiht sich damit den Buchstaben und Linien des Setzkastens
äßes, aber differenzierteres typographisches Aufbauelement
im rein materiellen Sinne jenen grundsätzlich gleich, ganz
stens im Buchdruck, wo dies durch die Zerlegung der Ober-
ssermaßen typographisch) erhabene Rasterpunkte und die
Schrifthöhe bewirkt wird. In den modernen Druckverfahren
Offset entfällt ein solcher Maßstab vollkommen; hier würde
gesetzte Meinung in der materiellen Form keine Stütze für
g der Ungleichartigkeit mehr finden.

Klischees in den übrigen Satz ist den Gesetzen einer
und einer harmonischen Flächengestaltung unter-
en die Abneigung der Buchkünstler gegen das
und auch der Luxusbegriff des „schönen Buchs"
ieht der Buchgestalter unserer Zeit im Photo-
benbürtigen Bestandteil des schönen Buches.
eines Reklame-Typophotos ist das nebenan
Piet Zwart. Hier begegnen wir zugleich auch
ephotogramm (papierisoliertes Hochspannungs-
ginnt das Wort „high" (hoch), das kleine L das Wort „low"
chriftarten und die schwarzen und roten Formen sind sehr gut
ausgewogen, das Ganze ist von bezaubernder Schönheit.
e die Wirkung des Photos zu steigern vermag, erweisen die
n dieses Beispiels. Die ebene rote Fläche des dicken L steht
Kontrast zu den zarten plastischen Formen des Photogramms.
Typographie korrespondieren in ihren Maßen mit denen des
tellinie von NKF. mit dem Mittelpunkt des Kabelquerschnitts,
der roten Schrift mit dessen äußerstem Punkte usw.

PIET ZWART (Holland): Werbeblatt. Schwarz und rot auf weiß. Format A 4.

7
97

13

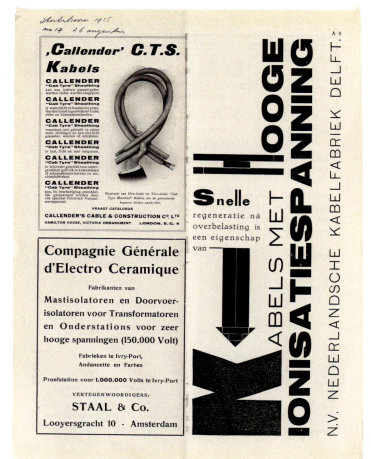

14

13 NKF advertisement by Piet Zwart
in Jan Tschichold, *The New Typography* (*Die neue Typographie*),
1928, letterpress, 8⅜ × 5⅞ inches
(21.25 × 15 cm), Berlin.

14 Piet Zwart, page featuring an advertisement for NKF ("High Ionization
Potential") in *High Current* (*Sterkstroom*), vol. 3, no. 17, August 26,
1925, letterpress, 12⅛ × 9⅛ inches
(30.75 × 23.25 cm), The Hague.

15 Piet Zwart, advertisement for NKF
("Hot Spots"), 1926, letterpress,
12½ × 8½ inches (31.75 × 21.5 cm),
The Hague.

These principles resonate in everyday advertising now but were radical in 1925, and Tschichold's ability to put them forward in a major trade journal meant they were well on their way into the mainstream.

By the time of the issue's release, Zwart had already begun establishing his place in the constellation of New Typography. Soon he struck up regular correspondence with Tschichold, and in 1928, when Tschichold published *The New Typography*, a more substantial and practical guide to the new principles, he highlighted Zwart's work for NKF. Discussing an advertisement leaflet for paper-insulated high tension cables, Tschichold praises Zwart's integration of text and photography, and, describing Zwart's use of elongated letterforms, he concludes, "The balance of the chosen types and the areas of black and red are superb, and the whole is a composition of enchanting beauty."[14] **13** Like his compatriots in Germany, Zwart sought to contribute his own views to the theoretical debate, writing an article entitled "from old to new typography" ("van oude tot nieuwe typografie") in 1930, and publishing two additional statements in the following years.[15] More important than any pronouncements, however, was Zwart's developing typographic practice, forged in this larger world of radical thinking and new possibilities, and resulting in a singular body of graphic work for NKF.

Although he shared, even anticipated, many of the ideals expressed by his international peers, Zwart was essentially self-taught in typography, an aspect of his development as a designer that helps explain his experimental approach from the outset. As he wrote when recalling his early efforts: "The first design that I made for NKF was hand-drawn. I was still not finished with it when the publication [it was for] had already come out. At that time, I realized this was not a very good way to work and then plunged headfirst into typography."[16] That very inexperience and the absence of long-established trade practices was precisely what allowed Zwart to approach print design with such freedom, learning by doing and finding his way, with some help from his printers, toward new solutions to longstanding problems of visual communication.

Zwart's early NKF advertisements for the electro-technology magazines *High Current* (*Sterkstroom*) and the *Journal of Electrical Engineering* (*Tijdschrift voor elektrotechniek*) were still based on hand-drawn sketches, worked up into coherent designs often employing different typefaces and line directions, as well as contrasted sizes. An example promoting the "high ionization potential" of NKF cables demonstrates this diversity of effects in a single typographic advertisement. **14** Zwart never lost that exploratory, playful approach, but his work would become more assured as he gained experience and familiarity with print technologies. A later advertisement from 1926 reveals the depth and complexity he could achieve from limited typographic elements. In this design, Zwart employs a massive bold *O* as both the letter *O* (thus completing the copy text disposed around it) and an iconographic depiction of a cable in cross-section, with the circular white counterform suggesting both a wire core and the dreaded "hot spot" that NKF products help customers avoid. **15**

15

In 1924, the company asked Zwart to design a pocket manual of technical standards for electrical cables. Known as the *Standardization Booklet* (*Normalieënboekje*), this small, vertical-format book, juxtaposing tables of figures and diagrams with striking typographic designs, demonstrated Zwart's boundless creativity with letterforms and layout. It was in many respects the culmination of his early experiments, reworking some of his earlier advertisements while also showing new designs in a series of bold typographic arrangements. **16** It also marked the beginning of a new phase in his work, not least in the use of colored inks for both text and ground, and the cumulative impact of successive page spreads—graphic effects that would be fully realized in the larger-format NKF catalog of 1927–28.

By the time he embarked on the catalog in 1926, Zwart's familiarity with the full range of printing resources had greatly improved. As a result, his designs became simpler, more refined, and, with a larger page to work on, he made greater use of unprinted white space.[17] Multiple spreads attest to Zwart's continuing experimentation with type and message (see pages 20, 50–51, and 68 of the catalog), but the overall design is leaner and more elegant and measured when compared to his earlier advertisements. Typographic effect is the governing principle throughout, whether seen in contrasts of type size, the deployment of diagonal lines of text, or the simple disposition of letterforms that distinguish the opening page spread, with its overprinted *NKF* in red and blue, and the cover design used for both the yellow paperback and the less common gray hardcover editions. **17**

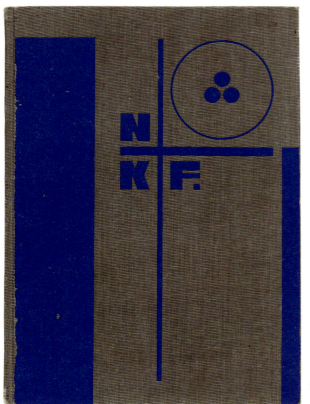

Faithful to the New Typography dictum, Zwart uses sans serif faces throughout, but as with many of his design decisions, his type choices make a subtle contribution to the overall effect of the catalog. This was not as simple as it might appear. There were only limited sans faces available at the time, mostly so-called grotesques (*antieke* in Dutch) or display faces developed in the previous century for posters and headlines. They may have been eye-catching, but they were often clumsy and inconsistent, especially when used for longer texts. Indeed, foundries were only just catching up with the demand for well-proportioned and adaptable sans faces, the most successful being Paul Renner's Futura, which the Bauer Type Foundry released in 1927. Since type without serifs was an unbending requirement among modernists, designers often had to fall back on less consistent faces like Akzidenz-Grotesk or Venus. It was not simply a matter of efficiency or

visual appeal. With so much text to organize, and in so many ways, Zwart clearly needed typefaces that were adaptable, modern, and in harmony with the industrial goods being advertised. For body text, he selected Typefoundry Amsterdam's Kaart-Antieke, a clean, horizontally extended face based on the earlier Blair, an Inland Type Foundry design first marketed in 1900 as "an exact imitation of the small gothic letter now so popular with engravers for stylish stationery."[18] Titles are set in a mixture of Amsterdam's similarly extended Annonce-Antieke and two regular-width faces sold by Amsterdam as Breede Vette Antieke and Breede Halbvette Antieke. A glance at NKF catalog pages 34, 38–39, and 48–49 reveals Zwart's sensitivity to the different roles each face serves, especially in the contrasts between horizontal and diagonal lines of text, as well as the relative weights, sizes, and colors employed. **18**

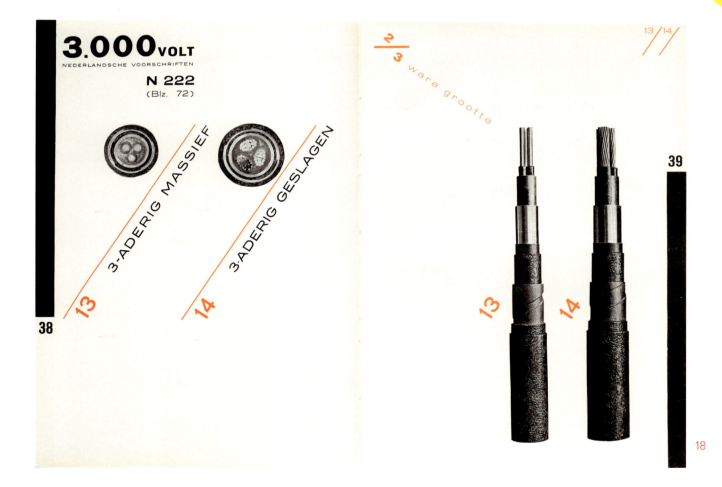

16 Piet Zwart, *Standardization Booklet* for NKF, 1924–25, letterpress, 7⅛ × 4⅛ inches (18 × 10.5 cm), Delft.

7 & 18 Piet Zwart, *NKF* catalog, 1927–28, letterpress, 8¼ × 11⅝ inches (21 × 29.5 cm), Delft.

100

DIE WELT IST SCHÖN

Fotografieren Sie?
Hier ist Ihr Meister

ROMAIN ROLLAND SAGT:

„Diese Bilder sind prachtvoll und eine Offenbarung."

FOTOS

Although these typographic choices are central to the look and the overall character of the NKF catalog, it was Zwart's use of photography that marked it out as a landmark in modernist design. He had already employed stock and commissioned photographs in some of his early work, but by 1926 he had begun to take a greater interest in photography. Again, Zwart was entering a world of new ideas, grand theories, and fierce polemic. Just as typography and architecture were undergoing a radical transformation in the 1920s, so too was photography, partly due to improvements in the equipment, but also as a result of new critical thinking. The New Objectivity (Neue Sachlichkeit), an art movement that emerged in Germany during the 1920s, rejected the expressionist emphasis on subjective emotional responses, favoring instead a detached, "objective" view of the physical world more in tune with science and technology. In photographic terms, this meant bringing a sharply focused, documentary approach to the subject or motif, as seen in the work of German photographers August Sander (1876–1964), Karl Blossfeldt (1865–1932), and Albert Renger-Patzsch (1897–1966), whose 1928 book, *The World Is Beautiful* (*Die Welt ist schön*), perhaps best shows the convergence of technology and aesthetics. [19] [20] But this possibility was not restricted to professional photographers. The launch of the Leica 1 (SLR) camera in 1925, and the corresponding development of 35mm roll film, placed photography in the hands of anyone who could afford the equipment. The small size of the camera and the quality of the lens also meant it could be carried anywhere, set at any angle, and used to explore startling new viewpoints, while yielding high-quality prints.

Even before taking up the camera himself, Zwart seems to anticipate the principles of New Objectivity photography in the NKF catalog, with shots produced in collaboration with the Hague photographer C. J.

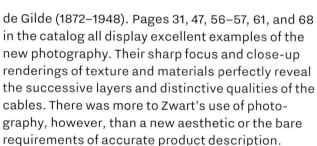

31

20

de Gilde (1872–1948). Pages 31, 47, 56–57, 61, and 68 in the catalog all display excellent examples of the new photography. Their sharp focus and close-up renderings of texture and materials perfectly reveal the successive layers and distinctive qualities of the cables. There was more to Zwart's use of photography, however, than a new aesthetic or the bare requirements of accurate product description.

Since the 1890s, there had been an ongoing debate within print circles about the integration of text and photography in books and magazines. To the avant-garde, halftone photography was an essential tool in the new age of print, and more than that, it was fundamental to the visual sensibility of the times. As Moholy-Nagy stated, "a knowledge of *photography* is just as important as that of the alphabet. The *illiterate* of the future will be ignorant of the use of camera and pen alike."[19] The preeminence of photography for illustration had appeared in countless manifestos, not least Tschichold's ten commandments of 1925. However, to the previous generation of typographers, especially William Morris (1834–96) and his adherents in the private press movement, the introduction of photography to letterpress printing was anathema. For Morris, it was an article of faith that letterpress required an equivalent relief process for illustration to ensure consistency of visual weight; hence the private presses of Europe and the United States placed a priority upon wood engraving.

The unity Morris advocated was still a vital force among artistic printers and bibliophiles of the 1920s,

19 Albert Renger-Patzsch, *The World Is Beautiful* (*Die Welt ist schön*), 1928, dust jacket design by Friedrich Vordemberge-Gildewart, photolithograph with letterpress belly band, 11⅜ × 8½ inches (29 × 21.5 cm), Munich.

20 Albert Renger-Patzsch, Cowper stoves at the blast furnace works in Herrenwyk, seen from below (Kauper, von unten gesehen. Hochofenwerk, Herrenwyk), from page 91 of *The World Is Beautiful* (*Die Welt ist schön*), 1928.

and was vocally defended in the specialist journals. It was the apparent dichotomy of letterpress and photographic imagery that so exercised commentators; while the text affirmed the page surface, the photograph implied depth. Yet this paradox was precisely what modernists like Moholy-Nagy, Tschichold, and Zwart were eager to exploit. Balancing the opposing elements may have required a certain sensitivity, but photographic illustration offered greater precision, apparent objectivity, and a new dimension to work with in the layout—namely, depth of field.

In the opening section of Zwart's catalog, one is thrust headlong into sharply receding factory interiors. Further along, on pages 26 and 29, viewers encounter photomontages of varying motifs and viewpoints. Zwart even employs photograms, images made without a camera by placing objects—such as cables and copper bands—directly over a light-sensitive surface (see pages 13, 15, and 17).

Far from disorientating, these contrasts present themselves as typical of modernity, which subjects one to multiple sensory impressions simultaneously. Speed, movement, juxtaposition, and contrast characterized the modern experience, and graphic design was a medium that could encapsulate this dynamism and put it to use. Perhaps only film could achieve more, and on a spread introducing railway signaling cables, Zwart plays on this very theme. A montage of an electricity-switching console, a series of abstract shapes suggesting rail signals, and two diagonal lines of filmstrip link the animate energies of trains, electricity, and movies, while a diagonal close-up of a cable on the opposite page seems to direct their movement onward to the next spread. 21

Zwart's use of photography is more innovative than that of most of his contemporaries. Not content with the supposed objective quality of the image, he freely crops photographs into circles, squares, and rhomboids, washes images in different colors,

and moves them around the page in concert with detached lines of text to create dynamic formal arrangements across two-page spreads. Yet this creative latitude never compromises the detailed illustration of the product. In fact, its results often highlight the specific qualities of the cables, their materiality and their mass. If Zwart's layouts share several features with animated film, they also recall El Lissitzky's concept of the "book-space," which in his words "must correspond to the tensions and pressures of content."[20] Both Zwart and Lissitzky trained initially as architects, and one might presume that their visual sensibility was shaped as much by an awareness of space, real or virtual, as by the disposition of forms on a flat surface. On opening the first page of the catalog, one encounters a world of new possibilities, a conceptual space akin to the three-dimensional exploration of a building or environment, all of which is created by the designer's handling of text, layout, and photographic imagery. Zwart, more than any designer of the 1920s, developed these possibilities to new levels in the NKF catalog of 1927–28.

Zwart already enjoyed a rising reputation within the avant-garde design community, and the NKF standards book and catalog provided a comprehensive survey of his accomplishment. Examples of his work began to circulate and soon became enshrined in the modernist canon, appearing not only in Tschichold's 1928 book but also in illustrations selected by Schwitters for a special typography issue of the German art magazine *Der Sturm* (*The Storm*), as well as in numerous contemporary design publications.[21]

A series of prestigious invitations confirmed Zwart's status in the international scene. First came an offer to join the Ring of New Advertising Designers (Ring neuer Werbegestalter), an association of progressive designers formed by Schwitters and

21

21 Piet Zwart, *NKF Catalog*, 1927–28, letterpress, 8½ × 11⅝ inches (21.5 × 29.5 cm), Delft.
22 Piet Zwart, page proof for *Netherlands Cable Works, Delft* (English-language catalog for NKF), 1929, letterpress, 8¼ × 11⅝ inches (21 × 29.5 cm), Delft.

the German graphic artist Robert Michel. The Ring included many of the finest graphic designers in Germany, and in the spring of 1928, Schwitters wrote to Zwart: "You have been elected unanimously, which shows the great trust we have in you."[22] Over twenty examples of Zwart's designs, including the NKF catalog, appeared in the Ring's exhibitions, which traveled throughout Germany and the Netherlands between 1929 and 1931.

In October 1929, Bauhaus director Hannes Meyer invited Zwart to run the advertising and typography workshops at the school, now located in Dessau, Germany. Zwart did not take up this offer, but he did teach a course at the Bauhaus in December 1929, which influenced his later views on design education. Finally, in 1929 Zwart was invited to participate in an exhibition and publication entitled *Captured Glance* (*Gefesselter Blick*) surveying the most important new developments in graphic design.

The book's editors requested a few examples each from twenty-six designers, including Moholy-Nagy, Tschichold, and Lissitzky. Zwart contributed five items, including an NKF advertisement for copper wires, strips, and cables ("koper draad, strip, kabel") and a curiously combative statement of his views on design, set in lowercase type:

how do i work? always with the thought that what we do is all rubbish and that it has nothing to do with a new design. the new design (the elemental one) is not made or revealed by individuals, at least the future form is not. i hope to once again have the opportunity to sit under a linotype for a week and listen to the rhythm there to eradicate my baroque tendency. because that is the modern plague. . . . everything smells like that fervent desire for form, a cheap and pretentious surrogate for the simple, sincere attitude toward life.[23]

33

Amid this heightened critical attention, Zwart received design work from a range of new sources. In 1930, the Netherlands Postal Service (Staatsbedrijf der Posterijen, Telegrafie, en Telefonie; PTT) commissioned a children's book, *The PTT Book* (*Het boek van PTT*); the furnishing supplier, Bruynzeel, began commissioning calendars and stationery; and Zwart designed photomontage covers for a series of books on film published by W. L. & J. Brusse of Rotterdam. Zwart continued working for NKF, producing a steady stream of typographic advertisements and completing a 1929 English edition of the catalog featuring new photomontages. **22** In 1933, Zwart finished a second catalog for the company, *Delft Cables* (*Delft Kabels*), replete with original photographs in layouts depicting every stage of the cable production process. This book was in certain respects a combination of the 1924 *Standardization Booklet* and the subsequent 1927–28 catalog, insofar as it combined many pages of factual information and tabulated figures, as well as Zwart's more freely composed large-format designs. It is a substantial piece of work, but it would be Zwart's swan song with NKF. Whether due to his expanding network of friends or simply changing circumstances, he was becoming more outspoken on matters of design, politics, and society. In 1933 he was dismissed from his teaching position at the Academy of Fine Arts and Technical Sciences in Rotterdam (now Willem de Koonig Academie). One

might assume that similar problems arose at the cable factory.[24] NKF maintained its commitment to Zwart's over all design policy, appointing Frits Stapel (1910–87), one of his followers, as his successor. Stapel continued to develop the firm's graphic identity, even using some of Zwart's photographs and designs into the 1950s. In the meantime, Zwart began a new phase in his career, returning increasingly to furniture and interior design. In terms of his graphics, *The PTT Book* marked a new departure in principles and technique with its appearance in 1938. **23** But this was a far cry from the heroic years of the mid-1920s, a critical moment when many felt that the New Typography could change the sensibility and mindset of the modern observer.

Zwart's contribution to this movement is unquestionable, but it depended on the willing cooperation of his client. In 1923, when he began working for NKF, he had the privilege of a blank sheet on which to impress his ideas. NKF was a young company, and Zwart was left to his own devices to invent a new form of advertising appropriate for its products. The freedom he enjoyed allowed his skills as a graphic designer to develop without diminishing his experimental approach to the printer's materials. The NKF catalog was the culmination of this process, a masterpiece of visual communication, and one of the finest expressions of modernism in graphic design.

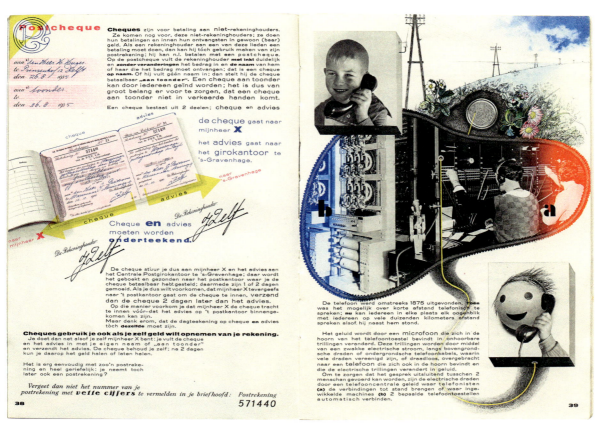

23 Piet Zwart, *The PTT Book* (*Het boek van PTT*), 1938, rotogravure, 9⅞ × 7 inches (25 × 17.75 cm), Leiden.

Endnotes

1 Piet Zwart, interview with Kees Broos (1970), in *Piet Zwart* (The Hague: Haags Gemeentemuseum, 1973), 6.

2 Piet Zwart, quoted in Yvonne Brentjens, *Piet Zwart 1885–1977: Vormingenieur* (Zwolle, Netherlands: Waanders/Gemeentemuseum den Haag, 2008), 66.

3 Piet Zwart, lecture at the Hague Art Circle (Haagse Kunstkring), 24 April 1919, quoted in Broos, *Piet Zwart*, 16.

4 See *Piet Zwart: Typotekt*, catalog no. 257 (Amsterdam: Stedelijk Museum, 1961).

5 In some impressions, faint lines within the green field indicate how the space bars were assembled to create a larger printed surface.

6 Piet Zwart, quoted in Kees Broos, *Mondriaan, De Stijl en de nieuwe typografie* (Amsterdam: De Buitenkant; The Hague: Museum van het Boek, 1994), 62.

7 See, for example, Ellen Lupton, "Piet Zwart: Three Advertisements, 1922 and 1923," in *Engineer, Agitator, Constructor: The Artist Reinvented 1918–1939*, ed. Jodi Hauptman and Adrian Sudhalter (New York: MoMA, 2020), 239.

8 Zwart's correspondence with Jan Tschichold, now held at the Getty Research Institute, contains frequent comments on recent movies. In a letter dated 20 October 1927, Tschichold writes that Fritz Lang's *Metropolis* is "one of the worst films of all time" (quoted in Christopher Burke, *Active Literature: Jan Tschichold and the New Typography* [London: Hyphen Press, 1994], 84).

9 Originally "constructed" (as the book's colophon puts it) in 1920 at the Soviet art institute UNOVIS (Utverditeli Novogo Iskusstva; Affirmers of New Art) in Vitebsk, *About Two Squares* was first published in Berlin in April 1922. Theo van Doesburg arranged for a Dutch edition to be published the same year under the auspices of De Stijl. It was in connection with this, and a traveling exhibition of Russian art at the Stedelijk Museum in Amsterdam, that El Lissitzky was drawn to the Netherlands in May 1923, thus opening channels of communication with Zwart and the new generation of artist-designers. Lissitzky also presented Zwart with a copy of *For the Voice* (*Dlia Golosa*, 1923), an equally innovative book of poems by Vladimir Mayakovsky with innovative typographic designs by Lissitzky, which also had an impact on Zwart's graphics.

10 The choice of Weimar, where the Bauhaus was located until 1925, was not coincidental. Theo van Doesburg had sought a position at the school but grew hostile to the expressionist ethos among the faculty. To demonstrate his opposition, he held classes in the town that attracted several Bauhaus students. Part of the aims of the Congress was to unite Dadaists and constructivists in their opposition to expressionism.

11 László Moholy-Nagy, "Die neue Typographie," in *Staatliches Bauhaus in Weimar 1919–1923* (Weimar: Bauhaus Verlag, 1923), 141.

12 See El Lissitzky, "Topographie der Typographie," *Merz* 4 (July 1923): 47; Kurt Schwitters, "Thesen uber Typographie," *Merz* 11 (November 1924): 91; Max Burchartz, "Gestaltung der Reklame," *Flugblätter mit dem Buntquadrat* 1 (June 1924); El Lissitzky, "Typographische Tatsachen," *Gutenberg Festschrift*, ed. Alois Ruppel (Mainz, Germany: Verlag der Gutenberg-Gesellschaft, 1925); and László Moholy-Nagy, *Malerei, Fotographie, Film*, Bauhausbücher 8 (Munich: Albert Langen, 1925). For translations of these and other early statements of the New Typography, see Paul Stirton, *Jan Tschichold and the New Typography: Graphic Design Between the World Wars* (New Haven, CT: Yale University Press, 2019).

13 Jan Tschichold, ed., *Typographische Mitteilungen*, special issue "elementare typographie," 22.10 (October 1925). Tschichold's first name appears as "Ivan" on the cover and as "Iwan" inside.

14 Jan Tschichold, *The New Typography: A Handbook for Modern Designers*, trans. Ruari McLean (Berkeley: University of California Press, 1995), 93–95.

15 Part of a promotional booklet designed for Drukkerij Trio, Zwart's printers for the 1927–28 NKF catalog and other designs for the company, "from old to new typography" was not published. For an English-language translation of this essay, see pages 38–47 of the present book. For Zwart's other typographic essays from the 1930s, see Gerard Kiljan, Paul Schuitema, and Piet Zwart, "foto als beeldend element in de reclame" ("photography as a visual element in advertising"), *Officieel Orgaan van het Genootschap voor Reclame* 2.11 (November 1933): 429–38; and Zwart, "Het typografisch gezicht van nu en functionele typografie" ("Today's Typographic Face and Functional Typography"), *Prisma der Kunsten* 3 (1937): 76–84.

16 Piet Zwart, quoted in Alston W. Purvis, *Dutch Graphic Design, 1918–1945* (New York: Van Nostrand Reinhold, 1992), 66.

17 The NKF catalog was one of the earliest publications produced on the new Dutch standard A4 paper size.

18 Advertisement for the Inland Type Foundry, *Inland Printer* 26.2 (November 1900): 333.

19 László Moholy-Nagy, "A New Instrument of Vision," in *Moholy-Nagy: An Anthology*, ed. Richard Kostelanetz (New York: Da Capo Press, 1970), 54. Moholy-Nagy's essay was written in 1932 and first published in *Telehor* (1936).

20 See El Lissitzky, "Topographie der Typographie (Topography of Typography)," in *Jan Tschichold and the New Typography*, 190.

21 Zwart's work for NKF also appeared in the Dutch avant-garde periodical *Wendingen* (*Upheaval*) and the yearbook of the Dutch Arts and Crafts Association (Vereeniging voor Ambachts Nijverheid Kunsten) in 1928, and in a 1929 issue of the German design journal *Form* (*Die Form*).

22 Volker Rattemeyer and Dietrich Helms, eds., *Ring "neue Werbegestalter": Die Amsterdamer Ausstellung 1931* (Wiesbaden, Germany: Museum Wiesbaden, 1990), 112.

23 Piet Zwart, statement in *Gefesselter Blick*, ed. Heinz Rasch and Bodo Rasch (Stuttgart, Germany: Verlag Dr. Zaugg & Co.), 108.

24 According to Zwart, his relationship with NKF ended in a dispute over possession of the photographs he took for the 1933 catalog; see Brentjens, 222.

35

PIET ZWART

FROM OLD TO NEW TYPO GRAPHY

37

About the Essay

Widely regarded as the first Dutch manifesto of the New Typography, this 1930 essay was included in a promotional booklet Zwart designed for Drukkerij Trio, printers of the 1927–28 catalog and other key jobs for NKF. The opening page of this innovative publication assures readers that by commissioning Zwart, the company "did not intend to demonstrate a preference for his working method or to spread propaganda for a certain typographical view" but rather "to demonstrate the capabilities of our typesetting and printing works, in view of the fact that his design places the highest demands on typographical techniques, especially hand composition." Nevertheless, the booklet did not make it beyond proofs, probably owing to Zwart's sharp polemic and his unconventional design featuring experimental overprinting, original photomontages, a collage of the printers' typefaces, and, at the back, new Dutch standardization sheets for paper dimensions.

By 1930 Zwart was a seasoned writer whose articles on art and architecture, published with the byline **P■**, regularly appeared in *Het Vaderland*, the Hague-based newspaper where he served as editor starting in 1926. He opens his first public statement on typography in a literary register with imagistic descriptions of a world changed by technology. He then embarks on a whirlwind retelling of Western typographic history, isolating moments when type seems to come into its own and meet up with the spirit of the age. While Zwart's narrative draws details and illustrations from American printer Daniel Berkeley Updike's 1922 book, *Printing Types: Their History, Forms, and Use*, its views of both history and the present are distinct. Closer precedents for his typographic conclusions can

be found in essays by New Typography peers such as El Lissitzky, Jan Tschichold, Herbert Bayer, and László Moholy-Nagy. A bluntly racist comment on the backwardness of ornament echoes architect Adolf Loos in "Ornament and Crime." Although Zwart's essay is dense with references and allusions, its ultimate vision of a functional typography "based on objectivity and explicit or visual form" is his own, distilled from years of practice.

Consistent with Zwart's original proofs, the following English translation uses dots followed by lowercase letters to begin sentences (except when the new sentence starts at the beginning of a line or paragraph). Zwart discussed this typographical choice in a note printed below his essay:

the above article was set in licht kaart-antieke from typefoundry amsterdam.
an attempt was made to apply the principles of the new typography to some extent; to some extent: as it was not possible to fully implement the aforementioned principles with the existing typographical means, which are designed for conventional typesetting.˙the start of a new sentence is indicated with a dot; however it was not possible to position the dot in the right place, namely level with the top of the small minuscules, and the final result was therefore, also owing to other complexities, a compromise.

Alongside the present translation, reproductions from Zwart's proofs offer glimpses of the original layout. Figure numbers in the translation correspond to numbered illustrations in images of the proofs. Zwart's captions for these figures appear in translation at the foot of each page.

from **old** to **new typography**

a change is taking place in all areas of human activity, which makes our era one of the most remarkable periods in history. ˙we have new technical possibilities at our disposal every day. ˙the borders between countries are effectively eliminated. an airship crashes in the inaccessible ice fields of our globe: with the help of a bit of copper, ebonite, and singing lamps, the SOS signal travels through the ether, mobilizes nations. ˙somewhere a spade is stabbed into earth: in two years' time, 400,000 cars per year will leave the conveyor belt at this spot, zoom across the earth, and change the earth's surface. a platinum wire in a glass bulb: radiation passes through opaque substances onto light-sensitive film: the x-ray reveals the internal structure of opaque tissues. ˙a football match holland--south america: the images are already shaking over the ocean and while the microphone is still ringing with cheers of victory, papers report on the match with an illustration of one of the game's key moments.

a forest disappears into a factory and leaves it as soft, shiny silk items of clothing. ˙the search for coal initiates the fight against terrible epidemics: in laboratories, medicines are extracted that will cure thousands.

our lives change every day under the weight of these and similar technical feats, and our attitude toward life changes too, our expression of life adapting with us; perhaps because of us, but irresistibly and despite us. ˙fields of human creative activity interpenetrate; nothing exists in isolation. today's countenance is already changing under the global aspect of tomorrow. ˙clashes between two or more attitudes toward life characterize our era; it has a chaotic character that makes many doubt the value of these times. ˙such was always the case: the contrasts are perhaps just more pronounced today.

on one hand there's a kindly formalism based on earlier concepts and means of expression, on the other new creative activity aims at the exact spirit of our age: clarity, efficiency, spiritual tension.

typography, too, is influenced and has been fundamentally changed by technical developments since the middle of the last century; in this respect it is experiencing the crisis that forces all old professions to adopt new working methods and produce new creations. ˙typography is also one of the elements that influences and is influenced by the spiritual expression of a period; every era has its own typographical identity.

so has our era its own typographical method of expression. ˙the modern printing company is not like that of half a century ago; the old hand presses have disappeared or been demoted to

oude handpers

old manual press

de alleroudste gezette boeken zijn imitatie's van handschriften, niet slechts door de wijze van zetten, doch ook door het gebruikte lettertype.

gutenberg en zijn tijdgenooten pasten de gothische lettervormen toe (minusculen). 'later komen enkele varianten daarop (fractuur, bâtardes der fransche drukkers, schwabacher). 'de meestal in twee kolommen gedrukte bladzijden worden met geschilderde initialen en randversieringen

[specimen 1 — gothische minuskels]

voorzien; later worden deze in hout gesneden en meegedrukt: kapitalen worden met de hand van roode haakjes en krulletjes voorzien. 'asymetrische ordening.

geheel andere wegen gaan de drukkers in het renaissansistische italië: een lettertype dat een variatie is op de antieke romeinsche letter, de z.g.n. antiqua. met illustraties en ornamenten in zwart gedrukt en als één kolom per bladzijde symmetrisch geordend. 'pio aldo manutio ontwerpt omstreeks 1500 een loopende (cursieve) letter, zoogenaamde italic, hij imiteert niet meer de oude manuscripten en kan derhalve beschouwd worden als de ontdekker van het eigen karakter der typografie. **1ste moment.**

een kleine variatie op de antiqua, is de elegante, ronde „elsevier", ontstaan omstreeks 1600 (stamvader van het vermaarde boekdrukkersgeslacht was lodewijk elsezier te leiden; hij paste systematisch de u toe, die tot op dat oogenblik meestal als v gedrukt was).

de gothische variëteiten werden vooral en worden nog in duitschland gebruikt. 'in nederland pasten de drukkers deze lettersoort in

[specimen 4 — bâtarde]

de eerste eeuw toe naast een variatie op de antiqua, de mediæval (rudementen van het gothischtype vindt men nog altijd in het hoofd van enkele bladen: telegraaf, handelsblad). 'de overige landen passen ook in de allereerste tijd het gothisch, daarna uitsluitend de mediævaltypen toe. tegen het eind van de 18de eeuw ontwikkelt zich een antiquiseerende lettervorm, de z.g.n. fransche antiqua, waarvoor de stempelsnijders didot en bodoni de meest bekende typen ontwerpen. **2de moment.**

het typografische type wordt gecreëerd. 'het zijn klare typen met gevoelige zwellingen in de lijnen, voortgekomen uit het graveeren; niet meer de variëteiten op een geschreven letter. 'op deze klaarheid berust de veelvuldige toepassing van deze typen.

in duitschland streeft men er in dien tijd naar de „fractuur" meer en meer naar de antiqua om te vormen (unger-fractuur, jean paul-fractuur). het lukt nooit een vorm te vinden die evenzeer als de fransche antiqua dermate vrijkomt van de

POLIPHILO INCOMINCIA IL SECONDO LIBRO DI LA SVA HYPNEROTOMACHIA. NEL QVALE POLIA ET LVI DISERTABONDI, IN QVALE MODO ET VARIO CASO NARRANO INTERCALARIAMENTE IL SVO INAMORAMENTO.

NARRA QVIVI LA DIVA POLIA LA NOBILE ET ANTIQVA ORIGINE SVA. ET COMO PER LI PREDE CESSORI SVI TRIVISIO FVE EDIFICATO. ET DI QVEL LA GENTE LELIA ORIVNDA. ET PER QVALE MODO DISAVEDVTA ET INSCIA DISCONCIAMENTE SE INAMOROE DI LEI IL SVO DILECTO POLIPHILO.

[specimen 6 — bladzijde uit de hypnerotomachia poliphili]

[specimen 7 — italic van aldo manutio]

[specimen 8 — bladzijde uit elzevier's republica]

proofing machines; mechanically driven rotary presses fill the halls with their rhythmical beat; typesetting machines hail letter matrices into lines, pages, books, newspapers; the speed of this era resounds in typesetting and printing and hastens new methods, new possibilities. ˙these different methods have allowed for new forms of expression; in general they are still poorly understood or are adapted to carefully preserved tradition, or they have either only tentatively developed their own character or have failed to do so entirely.

but no field of human activity escapes the rebellious élan with which our era storms forward, and certainly not typography, which is connected to all expressions of life by thousands of threads.

the spiritual tensions of this period are transforming its mode of expression; each era has its typographical identity, ours is shaping its own. **✝**

the development of the old typography up to the end of the last century could mainly be seen in books, but also in the handful of newspapers. ˙it wasn't yet seen in pamphlets, notices, advertisements, and the numerous fields for which it is now utilized.

the oldest typeset books are imitations of manuscripts, not only due to the method of typesetting, but also due to the kind of type used. **1**

gutenberg and his contemporaries employed blackletter (minuscules). **2** ˙some variants emerged later (fraktur, bastarda from the french printers, schwabacher). **3** **4** **5** ˙their pages, generally printed in two columns, featured painted initials and decorative borders; later these were cut into wood and printed too: capitals were given red accents and flourishes by hand. ˙asymmetrical arrangement.

printers in renaissance italy explored completely different paths: a typeface based on antique roman script, called antiqua, with illustrations and ornaments printed in black and arranged symmetrically in one column per page. **6** ˙around 1500 aldus pius manutius developed a running (cursive) letter, called italic, and because he no longer imitated the old manuscripts, he can be considered the discoverer of the specific character of typography. **7** **1st moment.**

a minor variation on antiqua is the elegant, rounded "elsevier," developed around 1600 (lodewijk elsevier was the first in a family of acclaimed book printers; he systematically employed the u, which before then had generally been printed as a v). **8** ˙blackletter variants were and still are mainly used in germany. **9** ˙in the netherlands printers used this kind of letter in the first century alongside a form of antiqua known as venetian (elements of blackletter type are still found in the headers of some newspapers: telegraaf, handelsblad). **10** ˙other countries also used blackletter at first, then used the venetian types exclusively. toward the end of the 18th century a classical letterform arose, called french antiqua, for which the engravers didot and bodoni designed the best-known types. **11** **12** **2nd moment.**

typographical type was created. ˙these were clear typefaces with delicate swellings in the lines. derived from engraving; no longer variations on the written letter. ˙their clarity accounts for their widespread use.

in germany at that time people increasingly sought to turn "fraktur" into antiqua (unger-fraktur, jean paul–fraktur). **13** ˙no form was found that, to the extent of french antiqua, broke free from the faltering movements of handwriting, and so the germans did not succeed in creating a "typographical type." ˙the fate of fraktur was thus sealed.

today we are experiencing a decline of the blackletter "scripts" (the berliner tageblatt was the first newspaper to adopt latin type).

41

1 page from old dutch printed matter, an abecedarium circa 1473.
2 gutenberg "catholicon," mainz 1460.
3 fraktur used in 1479 by neumeister, mainz.
4 bastarda used in bruges in 1484.
5 schwabacher used by froschauer, zurich 1567.
6 page from hypnerotomachia poliphili; aldus, venice 1499.
7 italic of aldus manutius.
8 page from elsevier's republics 1627.

the "typographical type" of didot and bodoni marked the beginning of a new development in letterforms. ˙in the early 19th century we sporadically find the archetypical forms of what became known as the grotesque, a consequence of didot's principle insofar as all superfluous decorative elements, which his type still possesses, are excluded and an absolutely clear "general" form is created.

typography, however, like most subjects in the 19th century, encountered a period of decline; around 1880 its products were completely corrupted by coquetting with aspects of lithography (so-called artistic printing), the principles of typography succumbing to the same degeneration as, for example, those of architecture and applied art. **14** ˙the accumulation of meaninglessness, the violation of materials, the false pathos, the obscene gloss on one hand and barren sobriety on the other make this period one of the most tragic in terms of cultural development. ˙the typographer passionately employed lines and ornaments, spilled out vignettes, and within a single square decimeter gave an exposé of every typeface in their case, evidently wanting typography to appear as untypographical as possible.

around 1890 a few seekers emerged from the dull characterless still life. ˙after 1850 painting had taken a new direction; literature had liberated itself from the embrace of the rhetoricians; architecture suspected there were broader horizons beyond the artificial panorama of gothic cathedrals, ancient temples, and romantic villas; the peripheral fields, applied arts and graphic arts, entertained fresher expressions. ˙although the starting points and guidelines were usually chosen at random, new life and a new creative urge appeared.

typography also came back to life, answering the harsh degeneration of taste and insight of the day with more reasonable expressions.

42

morris with his hatred of machines and machine products theoretically and practically initiated a revival of craftsmanship in england, with an orientation toward the middle ages. **15**

the "jugendstil" movement in germany reacted against historicism. ˙behrens, olbrich, van de velde; hoffmann in vienna; de basel, lion cachet, dijsselhof in our country, later de roos and van royen, wijdeveld, purged the typographical conscience of meaningless ballast.

in fact, they pursued aesthetic renewal. ˙they had not reached the stage of renewing form on the basis of new opportunities, new demands, new materials, new functions. ˙their aspirations were governed by an aesthetic formalism or by individual interpretations and adaptations of the new opportunities and demands of our time. none broke free from historical memories. ˙one advantage was that in type, instead of producing stunted historical forms, people revived actual old faces to meet modern requirements (de roos, hollandse mediaeval). **16** **17** ˙ostensibly genuine and legitimate, but in essence sensitive, modest, they serve an old expression of life. ˙on the other hand some imparted such a personal character to letters (wijdeveld) that they had an irritating effect. **18**

the aesthetically designed book, the arts and crafts book, was coming into fashion. ˙born in the sterile atmosphere of the drawing room, it made a tasty drink for those who lap up beauty. it distanced itself from ornamentation, yet was decorative; it did not arrive at explicit design. it was just as foreign to the intentions of modern life as the drawing board on which it originated; between negative and positive is the zero point: **– 0 +.**

I ask you, reader, to reread the first part of this article up to **†**.

9 german fraktur type from breitkopf's schriftprobe leipzig 1739.
10 venetian from pater's dissertatio leipzig [1710].
11 didot l'aîné 1892.
12 bodoni parma 1818.
13 unger-fraktur 1795.
14 "artistic printing."
15 morris's troy type: kelmscott press.

stokkende bewegingen van het schrijfschrift en het lukt derhalve de duitschers niet een „typografisch type" te creëeren. 'daarmede is het lot van de fractuurvarianten beslist.

in onze dagen beleven we het verloopen van de gothische „schriften" (het berliner tageblatt was de eerste courant, die de latijnsche typen aanvaardde).

het „typografische type" van didot en bodoni is het begin van een nieuwe ontwikkeling der lettervormen.

in 't begin van de 19de eeuw vinden we sporadisch de oervormen van de z.g. grotesk,

Wisset, daß ihr nicht mit vergänglichem Silber oder Golde erlöset seyd von eurem eiteln Wandel, nach väterlicher Weise; sondern mit dem theuren Blute Christi.

nt & augentur commerciis artibus e Mechanicis regna, quæ ire in peius minui certum est, ubi quilibet e po o scitatur literas: raro mercatorem se

een consequentie van het beginsel van didot, in zooverre, dat alle overbodige sierende elementen, die zijn typen nog bezitten, weggelaten worden, en een volstrekt klare „algemeene" vorm geschapen wordt.

de typografie beleeft echter als de meeste vakken in de 19de eeuw, een periode van verval; tegen 1880 worden de producten, door coquetteering met het aspect der lithografie, geheel ongebonden (de z.g.n. vrije richting). dezelfde verwording van de beginselen der typografie als b.v. die der architectuur en de kunstnijverheid. 'de opstapeling van zinneloosheden, de verkrachting der materialen, de onechte pathos, de tuchtelooze glans aan de eene kant en de dorre nuchterheid aan de andere zijde, maken deze periode tot een

46 DISCOURS

Enfin, malgré cette gêne, l'observation des regles de notre poésie produit de moins grandes beautés que l'observation des regles de la poésie latine. Dans celle-ci, le mélange marqué des syllabes breves & longues amene nécessairement le rhythme: dans la nôtre, les regles ne prescrivent rien sur la durée des syllabes, mais seulement sur leur nombre arithmétique; de sorte que des vers françois peuvent être réguliers sans être nombreux, & satisfaire aux loix de la versification sans satisfaire à celles de l'harmonie.

Je n'ai parlé jusqu'à présent que de cette harmonie générale qui, par l'heureux choix, l'enchaînement mélodieux des mots, flatte agréablement l'oreille. Il est une autre espece d'harmonie nommée imitative, harmonie bien supérieure à l'autre, s'il est vrai que l'objet de la poésie soit de peindre. Pope en donne l'exemple & le précepte à la fois dans des vers imités admirablement par l'abbé Duresnel, & que j'ai essayé de traduire.

dati ne'pieni, *che non trova l'invidia ove gli emende. Ma forse più sicuro è ristringerci a dire che han grazia le lettere, quando sembrano scritte non già con isvogliatezza o con fretta, ma piuttosto, che con impegno e pena, con felicità ed amore.*

Tanto più bello sarà dunque un carattere, quanto avrà più regolari-

der meest tragische in de kultuurontwikkeling. 'de typograaf bezigt hartstochtelijk lijnen en siersels, morst met vignetten, geeft in een enkele vierkante decimeter een exposée van alle typen die zijn letterkasten bevatten, wenscht blijkbaar typografie zoo weinig mogelijk typografisch te doen schijnen.

omstreeks 1890 treden enkele zoekers uit het duffe stilleven der karakterloosheid. 'de schilderkunst was na 1850 op frissche buitenwegen gekomen; de literatuur had zich uit de omarming der rederijkers vrij gemaakt; de architectuur vermoedde dat er achter het kunstmatige panorama met gothische kathedralen, klassieke tempels en romantische villa's, wijdere horizonten lagen; de randgebieden, kunstnijverheid en grafische kunsten bezonnen zich op frisscher uitingen. hoewel de uitgangspunten en richtlijnen meestal willekeurig gekozen werden, kwam er toch nieuw leven en een nieuwe scheppingsdrang.

ook de typografie herleefde tot redelijker uitingen, dan de barre verwording van smaak

such as choose to seek it: it is neither prison, nor palace, but a decent home. ALL WHICH I NEITHER praise nor blame, but say that so it is: some people praise this homeliness overmuch, as if the land were the very axle-tree of the world; so do not I, nor any unblinded by pride in themselves and all that belongs to them: others there are who scorn it and the tameness of it: not I any the more: though it would indeed be hard if there were nothing else in the world, no wonders, no terrors, no unspeakable beauties. Yet when we think what a small part of the world's history, past, present, & to come, is this land we live in, and how much smaller still in the history of the arts, & yet how our forefathers clung to it, and with what care and

67

347. Morris's Troy Type: Kelmscott Press

9 duitsche fractuur uit breitkopf's schriftprobe leipzig 1739
10 mediæval uit paters dissertatie leipzig 1910.
11 didot l'ainé 1892.   13 unger fraktuur 1795.
12 bodoni parma 1818.   14 „vrije richting".
15 morris' troy type: kelmscott press.

43

en inzicht in die jaren voortbracht.

morris met zijn haat tegen machine en machineproduct, gaf in engeland theoretisch en practisch de stoot tot een herleving van het handwerk, met een naar de middeleeuwen gerichte tendenz.

de „jugend-still" in duitschland maakt zich vrij van historische trapatzen. 'behrens, olbrich, van de velde; hoffmann in weenen; de basel, lion cachet, dysselhof in ons land, later de roos en van royen, wijdeveld, zuiveren het typografisch bewustzijn van den ballast der zinneloosheid.

feitelijk is hun streven een aesthetische vernieuwing. 'aan de vernieuwing van den vorm vanuit de nieuwe mogelijkheden, nieuwe eischen, nieuwe materialen, nieuwe functies, zijn zij nog niet toe. 'een aesthetisch formalisme of een individueel willekeurige uitlegging en bewerking van de nieuwe mogelijkheden en verlangens van onzen tijd beheerscht hun streven. 'vrij van historische herinneringen komt geen van allen. 'een enkele winst was, dat men bijv. in het lettertype, inplaats van de verkreupelde historische vormen, echte oude typen naar moderne behoeften omgevormd tot nieuw leven riep (de roos, hollandsche mediæval).

schijnbaar echt en gerechtvaardigd, in wezen echter de aanleuning, gevoelig, bescheiden, aan een oude levensuitdrukking. 'aan den anderen kant geven zij een zoo persoonlijk karakter aan de letters (wijdeveld) dat zij irriteerend werken.

16

het aesthetisch verzorgde boek, het boek op de wijze der kunstnijverheid komt in de mode. 'geboren in de steriele atmosfeer van de teekenkamer, vormt het de smakelijke drank voor de schoonheidslurpers. 'het doet afstand van versiering, is nochtans decoratief; aan de uitdrukkelijke vormgeving komt het niet toe.

het is even vreemd aan de moderne levensintenties als de teekenplank waarop het ontstond; tusschen negatief en positief is het nulpunt: — 0 +.

Wie sel den hoghen dans verstaen
Dat nighen dat swighen dat stille staen
Dat sweuen omme ende omme
Dat treden van dat sweuen an
Die snelle hoghe spronghe
Die minne staet die minne gaet
Die minne singhet die minne springhet
Die minne rust in der minnen
Die minne slaept die minne waect
Wie mach dit al versinnen

ik verzoek u lezer, het eerste gedeelte van dit artikeltje te herlezen tot aan †.

....in 1914 wordt de oude kultuurontwikkeling afgebroken. 'de kwarteeuw vóór den wereldoorlog bezit reeds uitingen die de komende periode voorbereiden; de jaren daarna worstelen nog met den ballast der hardnekkige traditie. 'een nieuwe levenshouding ontwikkelt zich. 'vergeleken bij de sprookjesachtige gezapigheid van de oude kultuurperiode een winst, een verlies? het opmaken van deze

NOVEMBER 18

balans is niet belangrijk, zoomin als 't zin heeft te redekavelen over de waarde van 't anders-worden bij 't ouder-worden. 'we staan te dicht bij 't hedendaagsche gebeuren, om zijn tendenzen te kunnen overzien; zeker is echter, dat de klankbodems van het menschelijk leven: techniek, wetenschap, wijsbegeerte, geloofsleer, kunst, de spanningen reeds eenigermate reproduceeren en realiseeren. 'de menschelijke samenleving verandert in haar structuur, onze denkgewoonten worden veranderd. winst? verlies? de appreciatie hangt van persoonlijke verhouding tot het gebeuren af en is niet belangrijk.

ook de typografie ondergaat wijziging. 'haar arbeidsveld is enorm uitgebreid. 'behalve het boek „vormt" ze de couranten, tijdschriften, mededeelingen, reclame. 'dagelijks worden ons nieuwe bedrukte papieren in de handen gegeven. 'tot de ontwikkeling en opheffing der massa is zij een der actiefste middelen; feitelijk zal de realiseering van de kultuur der massa, inplaats van die, door een enkele lagen der bevolking, door haar mogelijk worden.

reeds luther erkende eenmaal, dat de uitvinding der boekdrukkunst „het schoonste geschenk was van god aan de menschen". 'van „geschenk" is de „boekdrukkunst" gegroeid tot een machtige factor in de verandering van de menschelijke samenleving, een dienende macht. 'opdat zij deze gave vervulle, zal ze haar vorm in overeenstemming moeten brengen met den geest van dezen tijd; de eerste symptomen zijn reeds te constateeren, beginselen zijn aanwezig.

in de plaats van de oude typografie, die naar de „schoonheid" gericht was, baseert zich de nieuwe typografie op de zakelijkheid en uitdrukkelijke of beeldende vorm. **3de moment.** terwijl de oude typografie symetrisch geordend was, de regels ten opzichte van een middenas op het blad gerangschikt werden en deze vooropgestelde ordening behouden werd ook indien ze feitelijk onlogisch was, ordent de nieuwe typografie de regels van links af en laat ze naar rechts eindigen naar 't zoo uitvalt of om een gewenschte spanning in den tekst te verkrijgen (b.v. bij reclame).

de nieuwe typografie werkt derhalve asymetrisch voor normaal leeswerk.

de nieuwe typografie is functioneel.

16 de roos' hollandsche mediæval.
17 ven royen disteltype; zilverdistelpers 1918.
18 wijdeveld, gedeelte van een oud wendingennummer.

44

. . . . in 1914 the old cultural development broke off. ˙the quarter century before the world war already held expressions that made way for the coming period; the years after still struggle with the ballast of persistent tradition. ˙a new attitude toward life develops. ˙compared with the dullness of the old cultural period, a profit, a loss? ˙taking stock is not important, just as it makes no sense to argue the value of becoming different with age. ˙we are too close to present-day events to oversee their trends; however, it is clear that the sounding boards of human life: technology, science, philosophy, theology, art, are already reproducing and realizing their tensions to some extent. ˙the structure of human society is changing, our habits of thought are changing, profit? loss? ˙appraisal depends on one's personal relationship to the event and is not important.

typography is also experiencing change. ˙its field of activity has expanded significantly. ˙apart from the book, it also "forms" newspapers, magazines, notices, adverts. new printed papers are placed in our hands each day. it is one of the most active tools for the development and advancement of the masses; in fact the realization of the culture of the masses, instead of that of a few sections of the population, becomes possible through it.

luther once recognized the invention of printing as "the most beautiful gift from god to man." ˙from "gift" the "art of printing" has grown into a powerful factor for societal change, a serving power. ˙in order to fulfill this role it will have to align its form with the spirit of the day; the first indications can already be discerned, principles are present.

as opposed to the old typography, which was based on "beauty," the new typography is based on objectivity and explicit or plastic form. **3rd moment.**

whereas the old typography arranged lines symmetrically relative to a central axis on the page, maintaining a predetermined order even when it was illogical, the new typography arranges lines from the left and has them end unevenly at the right either as they come out or to achieve a desired tension in the text (for example, in advertising).

the new typography therefore works asymmetrically for normal reading.

the new typography is functional.

the old typography was decorative; it not only used ornaments, borders, and vignettes for decoration, it also gave the page (front page) a decorative flair through the use of various typefaces together. the new typography uses typefaces functionally; it focuses on the importance of "effect." ˙it has no need for ornamentation. ˙it also roots out the seemingly innocent remnants of the desire to decorate, lines and borders insofar as they are not functional. ˙as the civilized man overcame the tattooing negro within and regards the pure human form as beauty, so typography strives for purely functional form rather than tattooing with decorative elements or lines.

the new typography is fundamental. ˙it rejects a predetermined formal structure, but builds up forms according to the function; it constructs a page with white and black in a way that expresses tensions in the text: explicit or plastic form. ˙in advertising with its intrusive active text it employs all form-values that embody the compressive and tensile stresses of communication. ˙not only with black and white, but also with color. ˙in the old typography, color (the red of initial capitals, for example) was decorative, used for attractive effect. ˙the new typography incorporates active red as a functional element: as a signal, an eye-catcher.

in connection with its fundamentally functional nature, it calls for fundamental typefaces. ˙the embellished antiqua and venetian (fraktur is no longer present in our country) have lost their raison d'être.

we require more objective typefaces; advertising demands brutal legibility. ˙for now, the "grotesque" best meets this requirement; for now: the form is far

45

de oude typografie was decoratief; ze versierde niet slechts met ornamenten, randen, vignetten, ze gaf de bladzijde (voorpagina) een decoratief cachet door de toepassing van verschillende lettertypen onder elkaar. 'de nieuwe typografie past de lettersoorten functioneel toe: naar de belangrijkheid der „werking" eischt. 'ze heeft geen behoefte aan ornamentiek. 'ook de schijnbaar onschuldige overblijfselen van versierlust, de lijnen en randen, bant ze voorzooverre ze niet functioneel zijn. 'zooals de beschaafde mensch de tatoueerende neger in zich overwon en de zuiver menschelijke vorm als schoonheid ervaart, zoo streeft de typografie naar de zuiver functioneele vorm zonder tatoueering met versierstukken of lijnen.

de nieuwe typografie is elementair. een vooropgesteld formeel vormschema negeert ze, ze bouwt de vormen naar de functie op; ze bouwt een pagina met wit en zwart zóó op, dat de spanningen in den tekst tot uitdrukking komen: uitdrukkelijke of beeldende vorm. 'in de reclame met haar indringend actieven tekst past ze alle vormwaarden toe die de druk- en trekspanningen van de mededeeling belichamen. 'niet slechts door zwart-wit alleen, ook door kleur. 'in de oude typografie was de kleur (het rood van beginkapitalen b.v.) decoratief, gericht op een smakelijk effect. 'de nieuwe typografie verwerkt het actieve rood als functioneel element: als een signaal, een blikval.

in verband met haar elementair functioneele tendenz eischt ze elementaire lettertypen. de versierde antiqua en mediaeval (fractuur komt feitelijk niet meer voor in ons land) hebben hun bestaansrecht verloren.

wij verlangen zakelijker letters; reclame eischt brutale leesbaarheid. 'de „grotesk" voldoet over 't algemeen voorloopig het best aan dezen eisch;

TECHNIEK
techniek

TECHNIEK IN BOEKDRUK
techniek in boekdruk   **19**

voorloopig: ideaal is de vorm allerminst. 'hoewel er een zinlooze, bandelooze vermeerdering is van het aantal lettersoorten, door variaties op en „verbeteringen" van bestaande typen, werd een elementair functioneele wetenschappelijk gefundeerde lettervorm nog niet gemaakt. derhalve is de nieuwe typografie gedwongen zich voorloopig te behelpen met een keuze uit de simpelste, minst ver-

HALFVETTE
KAART ANTIEKE
halfvette antieke

KAART
ANTIEKE
kaart antieke

kaart antieke   **20**

from ideal. **19 20** 'although we are experiencing a meaningless, irrepressible increase in the number of typefaces through variations of and "improvements" to existing type, a fundamentally functional letterform with a scientific basis has not yet been created. for that reason, the new typography is forced to make do, for now, with a choice of the simplest, least adorned, most objective typefaces: several grotesques and a few antiquas. 'in any case, typefaces with a self-important, personal, particularistic flair should be avoided; their pretentious character conflicts with the essential nature of typography to serve; the more uninteresting the letter, the more typographically useful. 'a letter is less interesting the fewer historical traces it bears and the more it stems from the exact, tense spirit of the 20th century. 'every era had its characteristic type, and our era has yet to produce its own particular letters. 'these letters will need to be based on physiological optical requirements: not on individualistic reasons and tastes.

the new typography is shaped by objectivity. not by common sense, but by that objectivity that brought us the thoughts and creations of engineers: typewriters, cars, bridges, airships, generators, turbines, all the ingenious technical equipment of the 20th century. 'the engineer, this new kind of person, is using today's scientific resources to promote the reconstruction of all areas of life without historicizing traces, fundamentally, directly. 'this is the spirit typical of our period: profit, loss? . . . see above.

the critical spirit of the contemporary man continually separates the superfluous, uneconomical, irrelevant from the substantial and attempts to arrive at new forms of expression, new solutions; he seeks the greatest usability, the highest usefulness, maximum effectiveness. 'the modern typographer who takes these elements into account stumbles over his alphabet. 'why, he asks, do we have four glyphs for a single sound, why Tt *Tt*, Dd *Dd*, Aa *Aa* when his

19 vette antieke.
20 halfvette antieke and magere antieke.

typecase need contain only one: how many millions could be saved? ˙the typesetting machine keyboard could be half its size and the setup would be significantly simpler (the same applies to typewriters and signaling equipment: think of education!). ˙if we trace the historical origins of our letters it turns out the two cases are indeed two alphabets: majuscules or capitals are roman typefaces, characteristic of the use of the stylus: minuscules or lowercase letters are descendants of carolingian minuscules used around 800 and written by quill, which afforded a florid design. ˙in the renaissance in particular both typefaces were used together. ˙we still use both together. ˙why exactly? ˙the only possible reason is: habit, carelessness, idle thinking. ˙there is no logical reason to begin a line with a capital; aside from the germans, no other nation "finds" it necessary to begin a noun with a capital letter; the germans "find" it necessary. ˙we would find it inadmissible to write our year as M930; there is just as little reason to write Holland as there is to write hOLLAND.

the new typography takes these points into consideration. ˙from a practical and economical point of view, a single case would be preferable.

however, both cases are untypographical, especially the minuscules, which retain much of the character of handwriting. ˙both also fall short insofar as there are several ways of writing a single sound ch/g, ph/f.

altering these curiosities will, in the long run, only be possible by means of a collective will.

a phenomenon that goes hand in hand with modern economy, objectivity, and the production system is standardization. ˙in western europe and the americas, standards are being developed that, although at times lacking international validity, attempt to bring some order to the chaos on a national level (the standards of western european countries generally agree, because they use the same units of measurement). ˙it is only a start and is by no means complete. ˙but because

the practical and ideal advantages are so great, it is already imperative to give up personal preferences for exceptional trim sizes in favor of standardization in printed matter. ˙the typographer has to recognize standards as an integral part of modern print design.

the new typography embraces the possibilities of modern reproduction techniques and attempts to shape them together with set type: phototypography.
4th moment.

the old typography was "flat": static. ˙if it used woodcuts or other illustrations, it did so decoratively as incidental rather than formative elements in the typographic layout. ˙the use of photography (including photograms and photomontages) as an integral element in the composition means that the new typography has a spatial effect: dynamic. ˙it involves space and movement.

in general, the new possibilities are still poorly understood. ˙as in the old typography, illustration, photography is generally viewed as illustrative supplement, a duality. ˙unity between the spatially effective image and the flatness of set type certainly cannot be attained with formal decorative methods. it is precisely in the contrast between the two that the active element in the composition is found. ˙to present this in explicit form is the task of phototypography. ˙that it must exclude every historicizing letterform to achieve this aim is implied by the photo as an objective element typical of our time. ˙the miniature of the middle ages can no more be reconciled with typewriter script. ˙(a probably unintentional attempt to combine miniaturelike decoration and typescript was made with "congratulatory telegrams"; a more unfortunate effect is barely conceivable.) ˙when composing photo + letter it becomes increasingly evident that the most objective type we have at present, the grotesque, is most compatible with photography.

in summary: the new typography is diametrically opposed to the first typographical expressions;

then: contemplative (reflective),
imitative (mimetic),
decorative,
individual (personal).

now: active (effective),
explicitly plastic,
fundamentally functional,
collective (communal).

SELECTED NKF DESIGNS

Print Advertisements

Beginning with his first NKF commission in 1923, Zwart composed around 275 unique black-and-white print ads for the company. Most appeared in the biweekly *High Current* (*Sterkstroom*) and the monthly *Journal of Electrical Engineering* (*Tijdschrift voor elektrotechniek*), industry publications that launched in 1923 and were later consolidated under the title *Electrical Engineering* (*Electrotechniek*). The advertising space offered by these journals determined their two basic formats: a tall half-page column (shown here) and a half-page landscape (see page 55). Published next to ads from other companies, Zwart's designs vied for attention with competitors' symmetrical layouts, dense etchings and photographs, expressive hand lettering, and crowded serif type (see page 26, bottom). By opting for simple messages and eye-catching type arranged to draw readers into the act of decipherment, Zwart defined a brand image that invited, even depended upon, typographic variation and development.

This selection conveys Zwart's evolving strategies, from his use of large shapes and constructed letters as visual anchors, to his rhythmic arrangement of text on multiple axes. The advertisements also reveal Zwart's interest in typefaces beyond the sans serif grotesques of his catalogs, including such turn-of-the-century designs as the condensed titling face Neue enge Zeitungs-Grotesk (see "Koperdraad en Normaalkabel" on this page) and the script face Ridingerschrift (see "Mededeeling" on the bottom right of this page), as well as a typewriter-style face and, in one of his last ads for the company, Futura (see page 55, bottom).

1923

1924

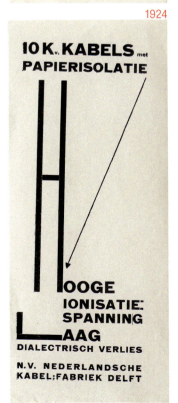

1924

19

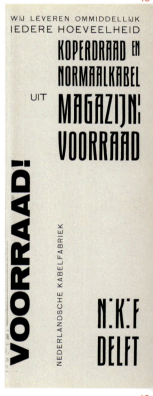

19

19

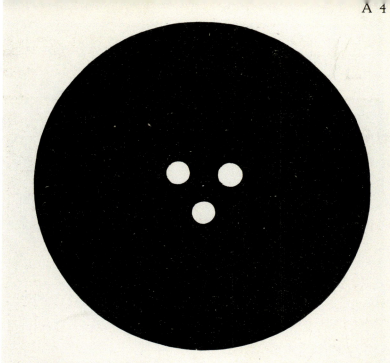

DELFT

IS VOOR VAKMENSCHEN SYNONIEM MET

PRIMA
KABEL

NKF

N.V. NEDERLANDSCHE KABELFABRIEK

DELFT

I. DELFT

NEDERLANDSCHE
KABELFABRIEK

VLAK_ DRAAD
ROND_ DRAAD
IN BOSSEN
N. K. F.
NEDERLANDSCHE
KABELFABRIEK
DELFT

KAB
VOOR
SPANNI

N.V. NEDERLANDSCHE KABELFABRIEK DELFT

VLAKKOPER VOOR
ELEKTRISCHE
MACHINES

ONZE D
gara

51

en

een SO

N.V. NED
KABELFA

TELEFOON
KABELS

Snel
regenerat
overbelast

1925

1925

1925

1926

1926

19

1925

1927

19

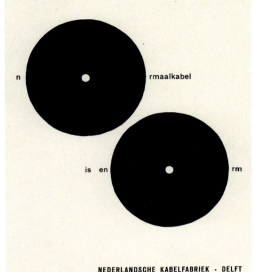

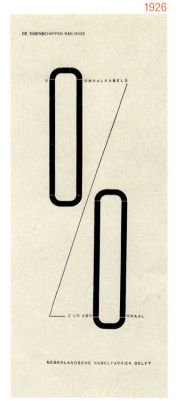

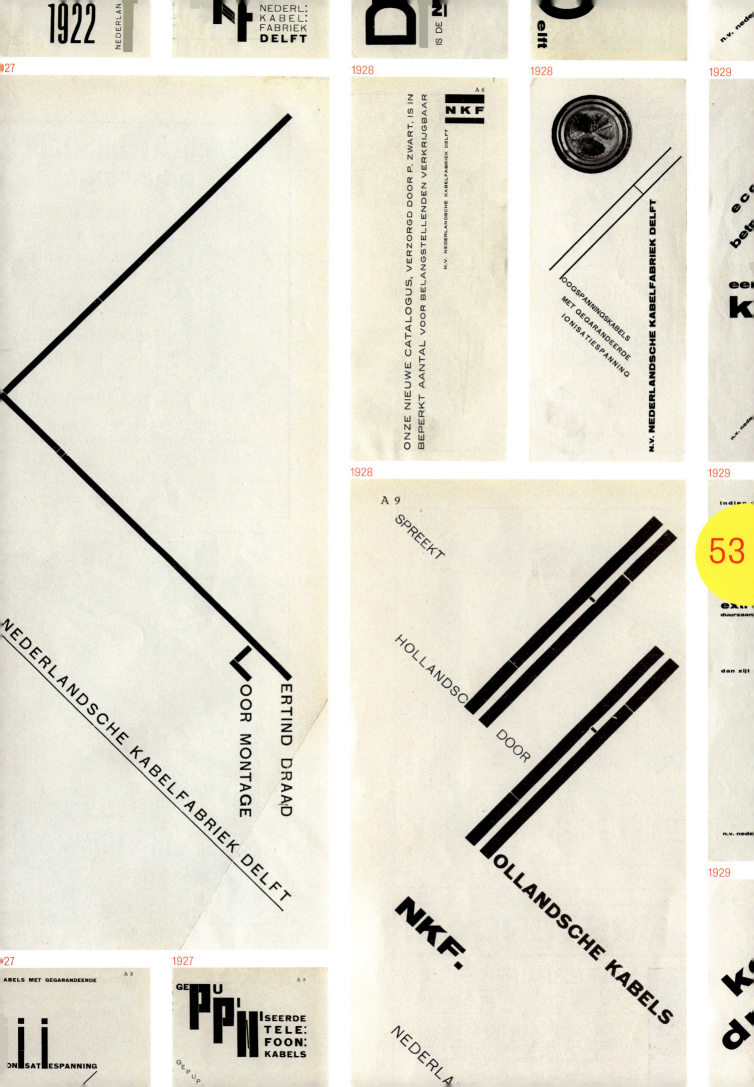

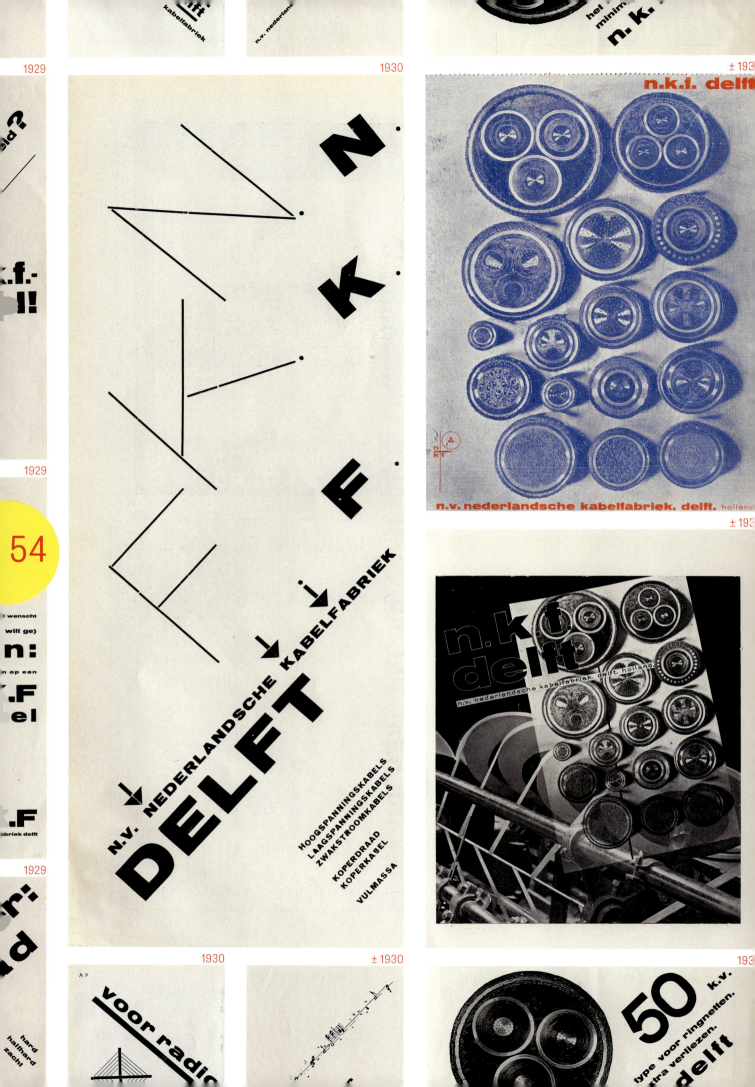

54

N.
K.
F.

N.V. NEDERLANDSCHE KABELFABRIEK

DELFT

HOOGSPANNINGSKABELS
LAAGSPANNINGSKABELS
ZWAKSTROOMKABELS

KOPERDRAAD
KOPERKABEL

VULMASSA

n.k.f. delft

n.v. nederlandsche kabelfabriek. delft. holland

n.v. nederlandsche kabelfabriek. delft. holland

voor radio

50 k.v.
type voor ringnetten.
tra verliezen.
delft

A 3

vulmassa vulmassa vulmassa vulmassa vulmassa vulmassa vulmassa vulmassa vulmassa vulmassa vulmassa vulmassa vulmassa vulmassa
vulmassa vulmassa vulmassa vulmassa vulmassa vulmassa vulmassa vulmassa vulmassa vulmassa vulmassa vulmassa vulmassa vulmassa
vulmassa vulmassa vulmassa vulmassa vulmassa vulmassa vulmassa vulmassa vulmassa vulmassa vulmassa vulmassa vulmassa

vulmassa
voor sterkstroomgarnituren
in verschillende hoedanigheid

vulmassa vulmassa vulmassa vulmassa vulmassa vulmassa vulmassa vulmassa vulmassa
vulmassa vulmassa vulmassa vulmassa vulmassa vulmassa vulmassa vulmassa vulmassa

vulmassa
voor telefoongarnituren

vulmassa vulmassa vulmassa vulmassa vulmassa vulmassa vulmassa vulmassa vulmassa
vulmassa vulmassa vulmassa vulmassa vulmassa vulmassa vulmassa vulmassa vulmassa
vulmassa vulmassa vulmassa vulmassa vulmassa vulmassa vulmassa vulmassa
vulmassa vulmassa vulmassa vulmassa

n.v. nederlandsche kabelfabriek

vulmassa vulmassa vulmassa vulmassa vulmassa vulmassa vulmassa vulmassa
vulmassa vulmassa vulmassa vulmassa vulmassa vulmassa vulmassa vulmassa
vulmassa vulmassa vulmassa vulmassa vulmassa vulmassa vulmassa

n.k.f.
delft

Standardization Booklet

Commissioned by NKF in 1924, Zwart's *Standardization Booklet* (*Normalieënboekje*) blurs the line between technical reference and company catalog. Bound in a stiff cloth case, its pages contain government-issued specification sheets for cables and related equipment beneath type compositions by Zwart. Tab cutouts aid navigation, and lift-the-dot metal snaps allow sheets to be added or removed over time. New pages appeared in 1926 and 1929, raising the total number of leaves in the volume from twenty-two to forty.

At the time of its release, industrial standards for cables were new in the Netherlands, the fruits of a commission established in 1921 to determine national norms for cable types and materials, size tolerances, insulative sheathing, and testing methods. NKF played a central role in the process and, with Zwart's help, made it part of their publicity.

Many designs in the booklet tout the benefits of standardization, linking NKF to the new norms and presenting these as a social good. An opening layout reads, "If even one consumer requires a cable that deviates from standard regulations, all are deprived of the benefits of standardization. Standardize!" Another advises, "Standardization frees creative labor from the burden of menial prep work."

Zwart's typography playfully illuminates the messages and prosody of his texts. Stretched ascenders and descenders, enlarged letters, sharp diagonals, and repeating elements evoke the charged and tensile character of live electrical wire. Shapes and letters built from modular letterpress elements bear outlines that reveal their means of construction. In one design (see page 59, top left), a tall constructed *H* and a squat *L* advertise the "high ionization potential and low dielectric loss" of paper-insulated cables, flanked by an early photogram of a loosely wrapped wire.

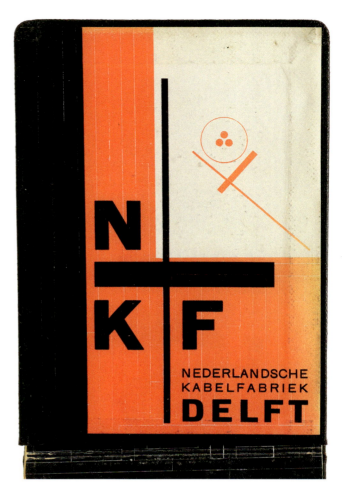

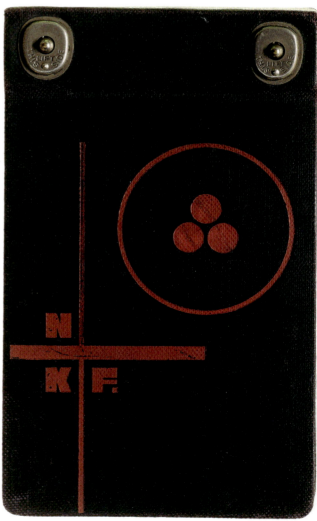

Standardization Booklet for NKF, 1924–25, letterpress, 7⅛ × 4⅛ inches (18 × 10.5 cm), Delft.

57

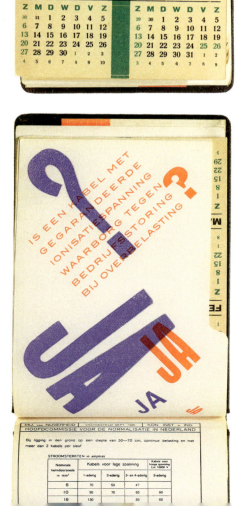

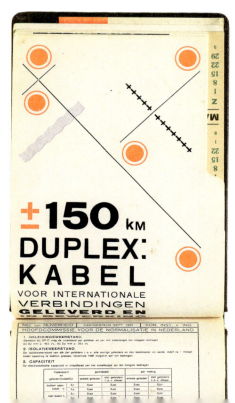

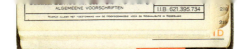

onze **Vulmassa** **Voldoet** aan alle gestelde eischen **O**nmiddellijk leverbaar uit **Voorraad**

FOUTEN SLUIPEN
KLACHTEN zijn ons Welkom

? gaarne! **Vraagt** ons advies

58

Hardkoper voor **Spanleidingen** O/vv koPEr kabEl. O/vv

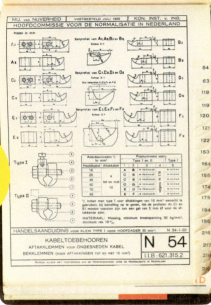

VlakKoper voor **E**lectrische **M**achines

GrooTSTe BEDRIJFSZEKERHEID N.K.F. Kabel

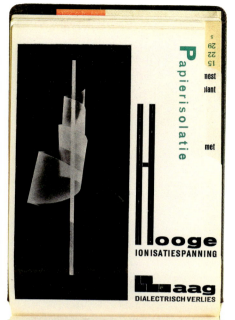

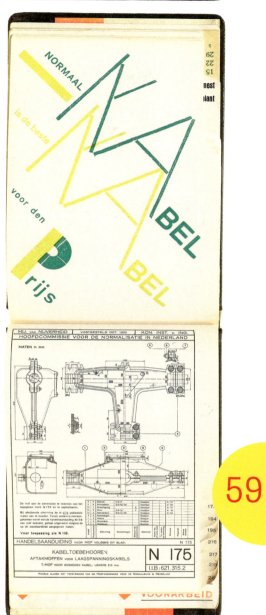
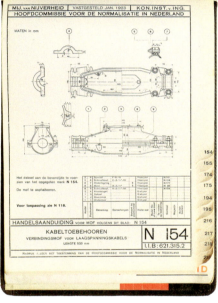

English-Language Catalog

Soon after completing the NKF catalog, Zwart began work on an English edition to support the company's growing export business. Published in 1929, this volume follows its predecessor in both format and organization. It also retains some of the original catalog's layouts, only with English text and gray bars instead of black on the outside edges of each spread.

The English edition is twenty-four pages shorter than the Dutch, reflecting the limited range of products manufactured to British Engineering Standards Association specifications, which appear in charts at the back of the catalog. Zwart nevertheless finds opportunities to introduce new photocollages, which help communicate the global reach of NKF cables and the company's industrial leadership in the Netherlands. Supplementing the Dutch edition's photographs by C. J. de Gilde, Zwart incorporates some of his own photographic work, including pictures of businessmen that animate a warning about cable failures (see page 62, top right) and an image of cable samples arranged like modern spires on a map of Delft (see page 64, top right). On one spread (see page 63, bottom right), process color printing renders the distinct hues of the copper, paper, and sheathing components that make up a telephone cable.

60

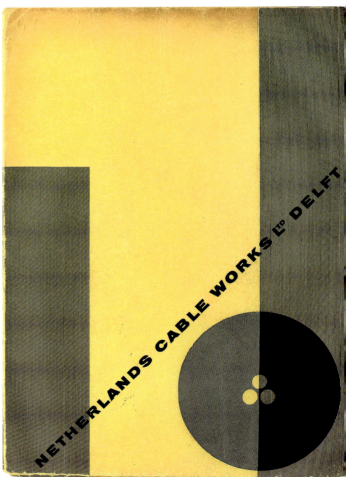

Netherlands Cable Works, Delft (English-language catalog for NKF), 1929, letterpress, 11⅝ × 8¼ inches (29.5 × 21 cm), Delft.

2

1929

N.C.W. CABLES LIGHTEN YOUR DISTRIBUTION TROUBLES

3

NETHERLANDS CABLE WORKS LTD

DELFT

HOLLAND

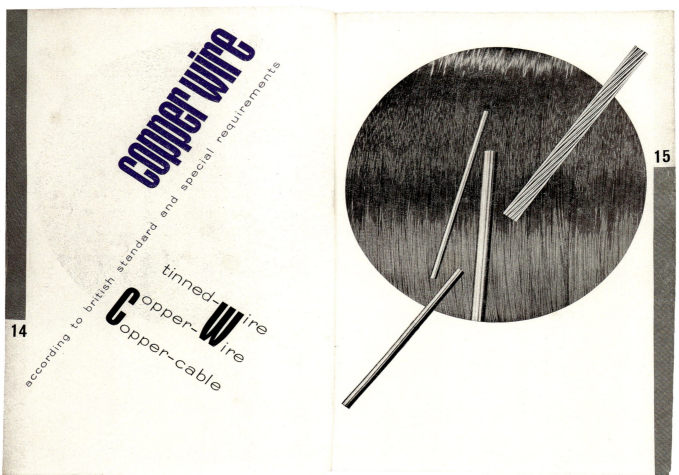

14

Copper wire

according to british standard and special requirements

tinned-**C**opper-**W**ire

Copper-**W**ire

Copper-cable

15

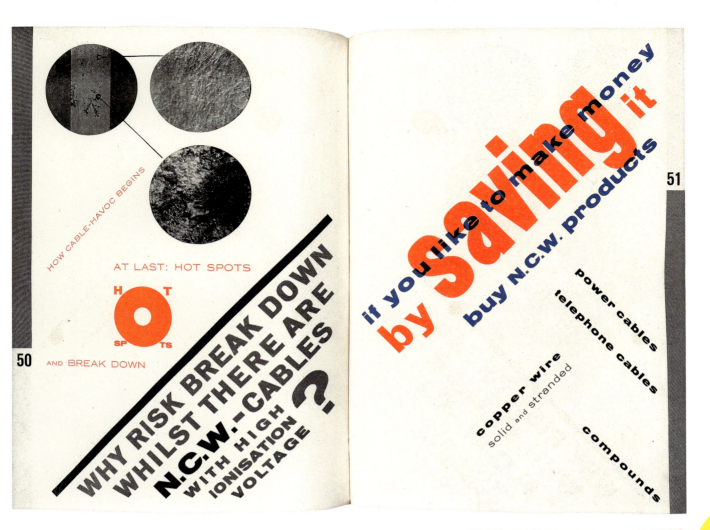

HOW CABLE-HAVOC BEGINS

AT LAST: HOT SPOTS

H**O**T SP**O**TS

AND BREAK DOWN

50

WHY RISK BREAK DOWN WHILST THERE ARE N.C.W.-CABLES WITH HIGH IONISATION VOLTAGE?

if you like to make money by **saving** it buy N.C.W. products

51

power cables

telephone cables

copper wire solid and stranded

compounds

TELEPHONE CABLE with high selfinduction

system **KRARUP** 15 x 4 x 60 lbs

52

53

54

55

Delft to-day: cable-town

64

compounds for special purposes
telephone cables for special purposes
oil-compounds
compounds for joint boxes and end boxes
filling-compounds for power cables

56

57

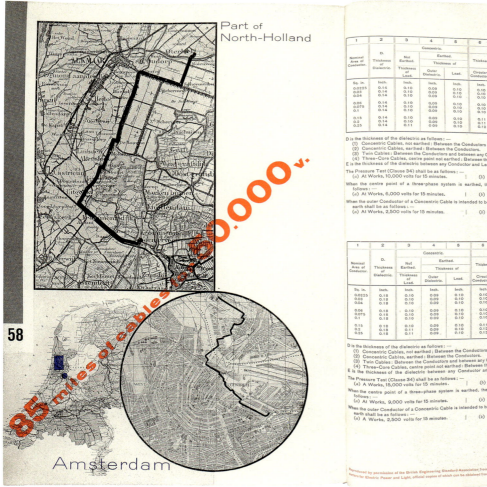

Part of
North-Holland

85 miles of cables for 50.000 v.

58

Amsterdam

62

3,300 VOLT PAPER-INSULATED CABLES
THICKNESSES OF DIELECTRIC AND LEAD SHEATHING

1	2	3	4	5	6	7	8	9	10	11	12
		Concentric.			Twin.		Three Core.				
		Not Earthed.	Earthed.		Thickness of Lead on		Centre Point not Earthed.		Centre Point Earthed.		
Nominal Area of Conductor.	D. Thickness of Dielectric.	Thickness of Lead.	Thickness of				Thickness of Lead on		E. Thickness of Dielectric.	Thickness of Lead on	
			Outer Dielectric.	Lead.	Circular Conductors.	Segmental Conductors.	Circular Conductors.	Segmental Conductors.		Circular Conductors.	Segmental Conductors.
Sq. in.	Inch.	Inch.	Inch.	Inch.	Inch.	Inch.	Inch.	Inch.	Inch.	Inch.	Inch.
0.0225	0.14	0.10	0.09	0.10	0.10		0.10		0.11	0.10	
0.03	0.14	0.10	0.09	0.10	0.10	0.10	0.10	0.10	0.11	0.10	0.10
0.04	0.14	0.10	0.09	0.10	0.10	0.10	0.10	0.10	0.11	0.10	0.10
0.06	0.14	0.10	0.09	0.10	0.10	0.10	0.10	0.10	0.11	0.10	0.10
0.075	0.14	0.10	0.09	0.10	0.10	0.10	0.10	0.10	0.11	0.10	0.10
0.1	0.14	0.10	0.09	0.10	0.10	0.10	0.10	0.10	0.11	0.10	0.10
0.15	0.14	0.10	0.09	0.10	0.11	0.10	0.11	0.10	0.11	0.11	0.10
0.2	0.14	0.10	0.09	0.10	0.12	0.10	0.12	0.11	0.11	0.12	0.10
0.25	0.14	0.11	0.09	0.10	0.12	0.10	0.12	0.11	0.11	0.12	0.11

D is the thickness of the dielectric as follows:—
(1) Concentric Cables, not earthed: Between the Conductors and between the outer Conductor and Lead Sheathing.
(2) Concentric Cables, earthed: Between the Conductors.
(3) Twin Cables: Between the Conductors and between any Conductor and Lead Sheathing.
(4) Three-Core Cables, centre point not earthed: Between the Conductors and between any Conductor and Lead Sheathing.
E is the thickness of the dielectric between any Conductor and Lead Sheathing of Three-Core Cables when the centre point is earthed.

The Pressure Test (Clause 34) shall be as follows:—
(a) At Works, 10,000 volts for 15 minutes. | (b) When laid and jointed, 6,000 volts for 15 minutes.
When the centre point of a three-phase system is earthed, the Pressure Test (Clause 34) between any Conductor and earth shall be as follows:—
(a) At Works, 6,000 volts for 15 minutes. | (b) When laid and jointed, 3,600 volts for 15 m nutes.
When the outer Conductor of a Concentric Cable is intended to be earthed, the Pressure Test (Clause 34) between the outer Conductor and earth shall be as follows:—
(a) At Works, 2,500 volts for 15 minutes. | (b) When laid and jointed, 1000 volts for 15 minutes.

59

5,500 VOLT PAPER-INSULATED CABLES
THICKNESSES OF DIELECTRIC AND LEAD SHEATHING

1	2	3	4	5	6	7	8	9	10	11	12
		Concentric.			Twin.		Three Core.				
		Not Earthed.	Earthed.		Thickness of Lead on		Centre Point not Earthed.		Centre Point Earthed.		
Nominal Area of Conductor.	D. Thickness of Dielectric.	Thickness of Lead.	Thickness of				Thickness of Lead on		E. Thickness of Dielectric.	Thickness of Lead on	
			Outer Dielectric.	Lead.	Circular Conductors.	Segmental Conductors.	Circular Conductors.	Segmental Conductors.		Circular Conductors.	Segmental Conductors.
Sq. in.	Inch.	Inch.	Inch.	Inch.	Inch.	Inch.	Inch.	Inch.	nch.	Inch.	Inch.
0.0225	0.18	0.10	0.09	0.10	0.10		0.10		0.14	0.10	
0.03	0.18	0.10	0.09	0.10	0.10	0.10	0.10	0.10	0.14	0.10	0.10
0.04	0.18	0.10	0.09	0.10	0.10	0.10	0.10	0.10	0.14	0.10	0.10
0.06	0.18	0.10	0.09	0.10	0.10	0.10	0.10	0.10	0.14	0.10	0.10
0.075	0.18	0.10	0.09	0.10	0.10	0.10	0.10	0.10	0.14	0.10	0.10
0.1	0.18	0.10	0.09	0.10	0.10	0.10	0.11	0.10	0.14	0.10	0.10
0.15	0.18	0.10	0.09	0.10	0.11	0.10	0.12	0.10	0.14	0.11	0.10
0.2	0.18	0.11	0.09	0.10	0.12	0.10	0.12	0.11	0.14	0.12	0.11
0.25	0.18	0.11	0.09	0.10	0.12	0.11	0.13	0.12	0.14	0.12	0.11

D is the thickness of the dielectric as follows:—
(1) Concentric Cables, not earthed: Between the Conductors and between the outer Conductor and Leac Sheathing.
(2) Concentric Cables, earthed: Between the Conductors.
(3) Twin Cables: Between the Conductors and between any Conductor and Lead Sheathing.
(4) Three-Core Cables, centre point not earthed: Between the Conductors and between any Conductor and Lead Sheathing.
E is the thickness of the dielectric between any Conductor and Lead Sheathing of Three-Core Cables when the centre point is earthed.

The Pressure Test (Clause 34) shall be as follows:—
(a) A Works, 15,000 volts for 15 minutes. | (b) When laid and joined, 10,000 volts for 15 minutes.
When the centre point of a three-phase system is earthed, the Pressure Test (Clause 34) between any Conductor and earth shall be as follows:—
(a) At Works, 9,000 volts for 15 minutes. | (b) When laid and jointed, 6,000 volts for 15 minutes.
When the outer Conductor of a Concentric Cable is intended to be earthed, the Pressure Test (Clause 34) between the outer Conducor and earth shall be as follows:—
(a) A Works, 2,500 volts for 15 minutes. | (b) When laid and jointed, 1,000 volts for 15 minutes.

Reproduced by permission of the British Engineering Standard Association from British Standard Specification No. 7-1926, Dimensions of Insulated Annealed Copper Conductors for Electric Power and Light, official copies of which can be obtained from the offices of the Association, 28 Victoria Street, Westminster S.W.1. Price 2/3 d. post free.

63

Delft Cables

Zwart's last major project for NKF, this updated catalog brings readers inside the company's rapidly expanding factory. Opening with diagrams of the plant and two finished cables, a series of photomontages shows each stage of the production process—from wire making and the application of paper and asphalted jute, to testing, packaging, and shipping. Using exclusively his own photographs, Zwart layers, crops, and highlights images of machines and materials, combining scales and perspectives to create technical illustrations that evoke the clamorous energy of the factory floor. The catalog's format amplifies this effect: In the first section (selections of which are shown here), every other page is trimmed to two-thirds width, leaving part of the underlying page uncovered and promoting interest in what the next turn of the page might reveal. A second section gathers current Dutch standardization sheets for NKF products, organizing them with thumb tabs and section icons.

Delft Cables (*Delft Kabels*), 1933, letterpress, 8½ × 7⅛ inches (21.5 × 18 cm), Delft.

de n.v. nederlandsche kabelfabriek te delft

biedt u dit boekje aan in het vertrouwen, dat het uwe belangstelling zal mogen hebben.

zij meent den velen, met wie zij gedurende haar bijna twintigjarige werkzaamheid een aangename relatie heeft onderhouden, de inrichtingen voor fabrikatie in herinnering te mogen brengen en de uitbreidingen te mogen toonen, welke de fabriek in de laatste jaren heeft ondergaan.

zij heeft gepoogd ook hun, die niet in de gelegenheid waren kennis te nemen van de wijze, waarop kabels voor het voortgeleiden van electrischen stroom worden gefabriceerd, daarvan een voorstelling te geven.

de ter beschikking staande inrichtingen naderen door voortdurende studie steeds meer de volkomenheid en dienovereenkomstig wordt het fabrikaat gelijkmatiger en geeft steeds grooter bedrijfszekerheid.

de beschikbare laboratoria stellen haar in staat de gestelde problemen volgens eigen inzichten en gebaseerd op eigen ervaring op te lossen.

dat op deze vertrouwd mag worden, meent zij in de afgeloopen jaren afdoende te hebben bewezen.

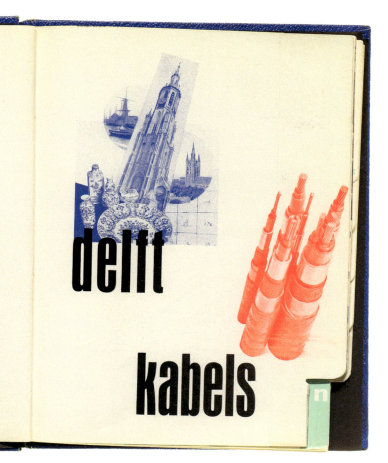

delft

kabels

de groei in technisch opzicht

wat wij konden:

in 1914 fabriceerden wij kabels tot

10.000 volt

in 1925 kabels tot **30** k.v.

in 1927 kabels tot **50** k.v.

in 1931 kabels tot **85** k.v.

en nu:

sinds 1932 fabriceeren wij kabels tot

150 000 volt

de groei in oppervlakte
1914 bebouwd oppervlak 5 000 m²
1932 bebouwd oppervlak 40 000 m²

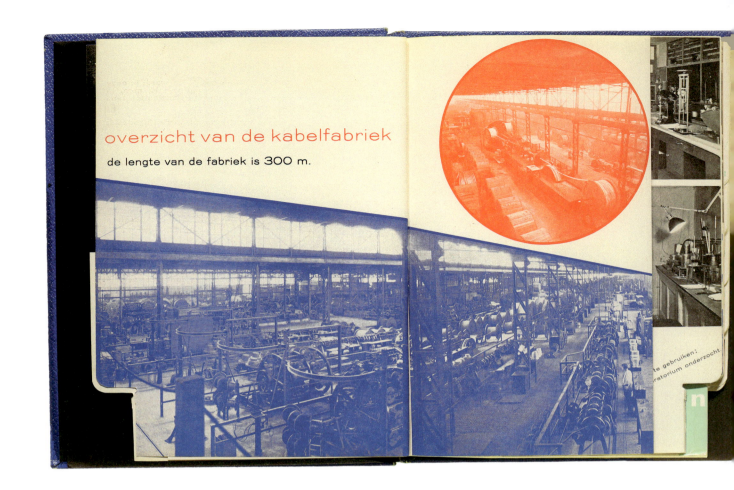

overzicht van de kabelfabriek

de lengte van de fabriek is 300 m.

te gebruiken;
ratorium onderzocht

walsdraad-
fabriek

trekkerij

wij leveren:
hard
halfhard
zacht
koperdraad
in de profielen:
rond
plat
vierkant

rond

plat

vierkant

een baar koper wordt
warm uitgewalst tot draad

het gewalste
draad wordt
koud tot dun
draad getrok-
ken.

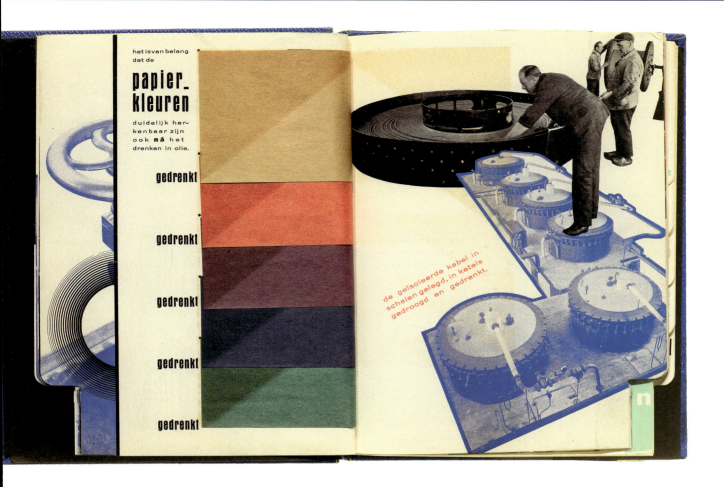

het is van belang
dat de

**papier_
kleuren**

duidelijk her-
kenbaar zijn
ook **ná** het
drenken in olie.

gedrenkt

gedrenkt

gedrenkt

gedrenkt

gedrenkt

de geïsoleerde kabel in
schalen gelegd, in ketels
gedroogd en gedrenkt.

**bepantseringen die
zware trek kunnen
opnemen bescher-
men de kabels.**

1 sterk en geheel gesloten

2 sterk; nagenoeg gesloten

3 minder sterk, doch gesloten

4 minder sterk, doch goedkoop

5 minder sterk, niet geheel gesloten;
kan voor grootere sterkte ook
uit staal worden gemaakt
(schachtkabels)

**de kabel wordt
met ijzerdraad
bepantserd**

óf:

met bandijzer.

het draadpantser
met jute omwikkeld

de kabel gekalkt

stroom

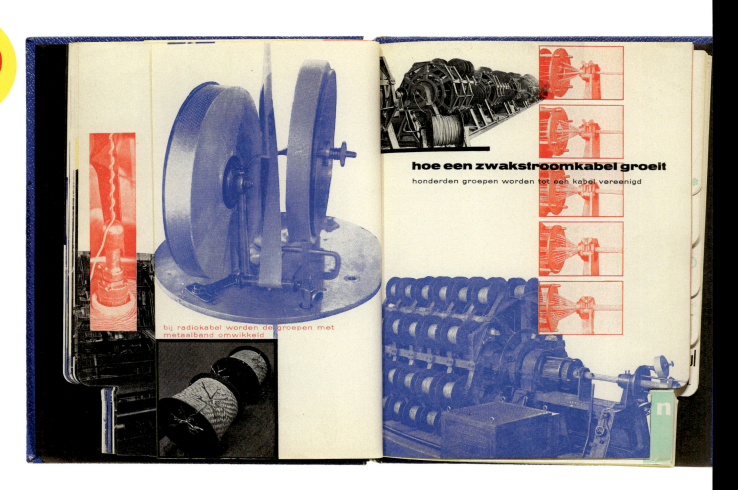

bij radiokabel worden de groepen met
metaalband omwikkeld

hoe een zwakstroomkabel groeit
honderden groepen worden tot een kabel vereenigd

de kwaliteit van ons fa-
brikaat is gebaseerd op
jarenlang voortgezette
laboratoriumarbeid.

de inrichtingen i
trôle en onderzoe
zijn een maatstaf
wetenschappelijk

oliekabel opgesteld voor
een proef van langen duur.

de vorming van holten
in de isolatie is de eerste aanleiding
voor een doorslag.

door middel van de stabiliteitsproef
(verwarming en daarop volgende afkoeling van den kabel)
wordt de vorming van holten vastgesteld.

de brug van schering
constateert de vorming
van holten langs electrischen weg

een vlakke karakteristiek
is de beste waarborg voor
den levensduur van den kabel

sinds 1922 worden de resultaten van deze stabiliteitsproef door onze fabriek
als eerste gegarandeerd
de waarde van de proef wordt thans
internationaal erkend.

n

hespelfabriek

expeditie

normaalbladen
gereproduceerd met toestemming van de hoofd-
commissie voor de normalisatie in nederland

koperdraad en
koperkabel

sterkstroomkabel

zwakstroomkabel

kabeltoebehooren

vul vulmassa
m.

zoolang één verbruiker
een kabeltype verlangt, dat
afwijkt van de normaal-
voorschriften, zoolang be-
neemt hij de voordeelen
van normalisatie
aan allen

n

TRANSLATIONS FROM THE 1927–1928 CATALOG

Zwart's 1927–28 NKF catalog contains three sections. The first (pages 1–29) introduces the company with a message to customers, factory photographs, and promotional spreads highlighting the component parts and advantages of its products. The second (pages 30–68) presents a full range of products—from high-current cables and telephone cables to weight-bearing reinforcements and a bituminous compound used for insulative filling. A final section (pages 69–77) reproduces government-issued standards sheets, which are referred to throughout section two. The present translation omits these technical documents, as well as the catalog's table of contents (pages 79–80), which repeats text from earlier pages. The first two sections appear here as thumbnail images, with the translated text set below.

1 NCW.
NETHERLANDS CABLE
WORKS LTD. DELFT

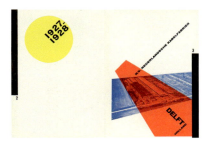

2 1927–1928
3 NETHERLANDS CABLE
WORKS LTD / DELFT HOLLAND

4 VIEW OF THE CABLE WORKS

6 NETHERLANDS CABLE
WORKS LTD / DELFT
Gone are the days when we would ask you to put our underground cables to the test, to risk laying a supply line from your plant so you could see for yourself that, with our cables, your grid would gain a reliable asset. Many needed convincing of the seriousness of our objective, and we gratefully seized the opportunities offered. / Much useful advice on your part guided us in our attempts to improve the product, and we were continually spurred on by our desire to be the best on the international market in Holland. / So we can now say that everyone knows: OUR CABLE IS GOOD. / This doesn't give us a sense of security, which is mere complacency, but instead gives us a sense of responsibility to live up to your expectations, and we ask you to prove through your support and criticism that, after a […]

7 […] relationship spanning many years, you are not indifferent to our industry. It would be an exaggeration to say that we can do everything. / Give us a chance and we will endeavor to prove that you will not be disappointed. / Don't just ask for the price: Your grid is only sustainable if the quality is excellent. / The demands of major clients in Holland are high: Only exceptional materials can be used. / Our smaller clients, equally welcome, enjoy these, too; there is for all: UNITY IN QUALITY. This means high reliability, even for the thinnest cable and for every short piece. / We exclusively manufacture cables with paper insulation and have focused all our attention on this since 1914. / The same level of attention is paid to every meter, and since we have been able to measure dielectric loss, this attention has, through greater insight, focused on the most favorable effect for ALL clients. / Orders for telephone cables suitable for international connections, subject to extremely high manufacturing and research requirements, show that the plant can also provide cables with nonimpregnated paper for all clients: UNITY IN QUALITY. / DELFT, January 1928.

8 VIEW OF THE COPPER
ROLLING MILL / VIEW OF THE
WIRE DRAWING PLANT
9 DEPARTMENT:
COPPER ROLLING MILL and
WIRE DRAWING PLANT

10 FROM WIREBAR TO WIRE IN
OUR ROLLING MILL. / WE ALSO
SUPPLY WIRE IN PROFILES
OTHER THAN ROUND.
ROUND / FLAT / SQUARE
11 PART OF THE WIRE DRAWING
PLANT / COPPER WIRE
PROCESSING

12 SQUARE AND / FLAT WIRE
SQUARE AND FLAT WIRE FOR
ELECTRICAL MACHINES

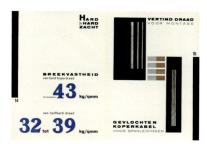

14 HARD / ½ HARD / SOFT
TENSILE STRENGTH
of hard copper wire / at least
43 kg|mm² / of half-hard wire
32 to 39 kg|mm²

15 TINNED WIRE / FOR
INSTALLATION / STRANDED
COPPER CABLE / FOR
TENSIONING WIRES

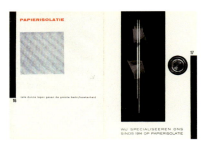

16 PAPER INSULATION
many thin layers ensure high
operational reliability
17 SPECIALISTS IN PAPER
INSULATION SINCE 1914

18 PAPER COLORS / ALSO
DISTINCT AFTER
IMPREGNATION

20 We guarantee / on cooling
of the cable / after heating a
flat / characteristic / but still
a flexible cable

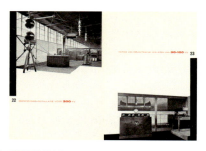

22 TEST INSTALLATION FOR
300 kV
23 MEASUREMENT OF DIELECTRIC
LOSSES FROM 30–100 kV

24 LIGHT

26 THE SECURE FOUNDATION
FOR MODERN INDUSTRY
27 DECISION! / BREAKDOWN
how much would a BREAK-
DOWN set you back? / use
an "NKF CABLE" and forget
the word BREAKDOWN

29 ELECTRICITY BUILDS CITIES

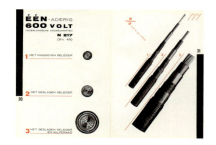

30 SINGLE-CORE / 600 VOLT
DUTCH REGULATIONS / N 217
(p. 69)
1 WITH SOLID CONDUCTOR
2 WITH STRANDED
CONDUCTOR
3 WITH STRANDED /
CONDUCTOR / AND PILOT
WIRE
31 [1 / 2 / 3] / ⅔ actual size

32 MULTICORE / 500 VOLT
HEAVY CONSTRUCTION
DUTCH REGULATIONS
N 218 / (p. 70)
7 2-CORE
8 3-CORE
9 4-CORE
33 [7 / 8 / 9] / ⅔ actual size

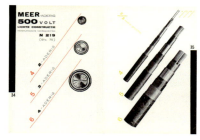

34 MUTICORE / 500 VOLT
LIGHT CONSTRUCTION
DUTCH REGULATIONS
N 219 / (p. 70)
4 2-CORE
5 3-CORE
6 4-CORE
35 [4 / 5 / 6] / ⅔ actual size

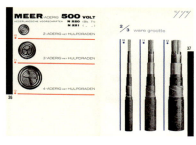

36 MULTICORE 500 VOLT
DUTCH REGULATIONS
N 220 (p. 71) / N 221 (" ")
10 2-CORE WITH PILOT WIRES
11 3-CORE WITH PILOT WIRES
12 4-CORE WITH PILOT WIRES
37 [10 / 11 / 12] / ⅔ actual size

38 3,000 VOLT / DUTCH
REGULATIONS / N 222 / (p. 72)
13 3-CORE SOLID
14 3-CORE STRANDED
39 [13 / 14] / ⅔ actual size

40 [15] / 6,000 VOLT / DUTCH
REGULATIONS / N 222 / (p. 72)

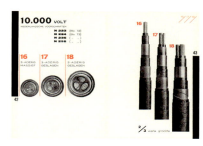

42 10,000 VOLT / DUTCH
REGULATIONS / N 223 (p. 72)
N 224 (p. 73) / N 225 (" ")
N 226 (" ")
16 3-CORE SOLID
17 3-CORE STRANDED
18 3-CORE STRANDED
43 [16 / 17 / 18] / ⅔ actual size

44 [19] / 6-CORE POWER CABLE
FOR 10,000 V / applied for the
SPLIT / CONDUCTOR SAFETY
SYSTEM / SPLIT CONDUCTOR
OF THE FUTURE

45 [20] / 3-CORE HIGH-TENSION
CABLE FOR 30,000 V / WITH
BELT INSULATION / FILLING
PURSUANT TO DUTCH PATENT
10822

46 HIGH-TENSION CABLE WITH
PATENTED METALLIC SHEATHS
"H" CABLE
47 [21 "H"] / METALLIZED PAPER
AROUND EACH CORE

48 [22] / 50,000 VOLT / SINGLE-
CORE UNDERGROUND CABLE
FOR 50 kV THREE-PHASE
SYSTEM / ⅔ ACTUAL SIZE
NO IONIZATION IN SERVICE
SPECIAL ARMORING FOR
MINIMAL LOSS
49 [23] / 50,000 VOLT / SINGLE-
CORE SUBMARINE CABLE
FOR 50 kV THREE-PHASE
SYSTEM / ⅔ ACTUAL SIZE
NO IONIZATION IN SERVICE
SPECIAL ARMORING FOR
MINIMAL LOSS

50 WE Don't want a "satisfied"
consumer / WE Want an
"enthusiastic" consumer
51 Tele / phone / graph

52 [24] / TELEPHONE CABLE
WITH AIR AND PAPER
INSULATION / 100 DOUBLE
CORE / DUTCH REGULATIONS
N 286 / (SEE p. 74) / 100
DOUBLE CORE

54 [25] / TELEPHONE CABLE
WITH AIR AND PAPER
INSULATION / 200 4-WIRE
GROUPS (STRONG CABLE)
DUTCH REGULATIONS
V 288 / V 289 / (SEE p. 76)
200 4-WIRE GROUPS

76

56 30-CORE TELEPHONE CABLE
57 EACH CORE IS SURROUNDED
BY AN ALUMINUM COIL

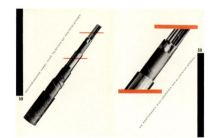

58 COMPOSITE TELEPHONE
AND RELAY CABLE
59 THE RELAY WIRES ARE FITTED
WITH ALUMINUM COIL

60 COMPOSITE POWER–
TELEPHONE CABLE
61 THE TELEPHONE CORES ARE
COLLECTIVELY SURROUNDED
BY ALUMINUM TAPE

63 SIGNALING and BLOCK
CABLE

64 a b c d e / PROTECTION that
can withstand TENSILE
STRESS
a for high stress; almost
entirely enclosed
b less strong, but enclosed
c strong and entirely enclosed
d less strong, but low cost
e less strong, not entirely
enclosed; can also be made
from steel for greater
strength (shaft cables)

66 FILLING MASS / DUTCH
REGULATIONS / N 52 / N 53
(p. 77) / diagonally sampled

68 Telephone cable / with High
self-induction / system
KRARUP / KRARUP CABLE
15 × 4 × 1.5 mM

80 [table of contents continues]
FOR THE ILLUSTRATION
ON PAGE 26, IMAGES FROM
"THE BROWN BOVERI
REVIEW" 1925 WERE USED
PRINTING: N.V. DRUKKERIJ
TRIO, THE HAGUE / PLATES:
BAKHUIS & VAN BEEK, THE
HAGUE / DESIGN: P. ZWART,
ARCH., WASSENAAR

[text accompanying
cartoon illustration]
Hi, mister, may I have that
bobbin when it's empty?
(AUSSI) [Australian monthly
magazine]

INDEX, CREDITS, ACKNOWLEDGMENTS

Index

Page numbers in italics refer to images.

Text Credits and Copyright

"Piet Zwart's NKF Catalog" © 1996 by Philip B. Meggs. "from old to new typography" translated by Alice Tetley-Paul.

Photographs by Piet Zwart

page 4: self-portrait as "man who thinks" for the English-language NKF catalog, circa 1928; page 6: paper insulation machine at the NKF factory, early 1930s; page 16: roll of copper wire with NKF advertisements, 1931; page 36: composition with metal type for the cover of a Drukkerij Trio promotional booklet, 1929; page 48: composition with sixteen cable samples for NKF, circa 1931; page 72: an NKF cable opened for examination, early 1930s; page 79: self-portrait with a telephone, circa 1932.

Image Credits, Copyright, and Sources

All images in this supplement and the accompanying facsimile volume © Letterform Archive unless noted. All objects collection of Letterform Archive unless noted. The facsimile volume is based one of Piet Zwart's own copies of the catalog.

All artwork by Piet Zwart © 2024 Artists Rights Society (ARS), New York / c/o Pictoright Amsterdam.

All other artwork still in copyright is registered with the artists' estates, heirs, or appointed licensing agencies. The publisher has made every attempt to locate the proper heirs and agencies for artwork still in copyright. Please contact Letterform Archive Books with any questions or corrections pertaining to credit or copyright.

page 4: Image courtesy and collection of Nederlands Fotomuseum; page 6: Image courtesy and collection of Nederlands Fotomuseum; page 18, top: Image courtesy and collection of Paul Stirton; page 19, left: Collection of Kunstmuseum Den Haag; page 20: Digital Image © The Museum of Modern Art / Licensed by SCALA / Art Resource, NY; page 21, top: Image courtesy and collection of Kunsthaus Zürich; page 23, left: Image courtesy and collection of Art Institute of Chicago; page 24, top: Collection of Bauhaus-Archiv Berlin; page 30: Image courtesy and collection of The Getty Research Institute; page 31: Image courtesy and collection of the Getty Research Institute; page 32: © Albert Renger-Patzsch / Archiv Ann u. Jürgen Wilde, Zülpich / Artists Rights Society (ARS), New York, 2024; page 36: Image courtesy and collection of Nederlands Fotomuseum; pages 39–40, 43–44, and 46: Images courtesy and collection of Huis van het boek; page 48: Image courtesy and collection of Nederlands Fotomuseum; pages 60–65: Images courtesy and collection of Merrill C. Berman; pages 72 and 79: Images courtesy and collection of Nederlands Fotomuseum

About the Contributors

Philip B. Meggs was a design history scholar and a professor in the Communication Arts and Design Department at Virginia Commonwealth University. His 1983 book, *A History of Graphic Design* (retitled *Meggs' History of Graphic Design* in 2006), set the standard for surveys of graphic design history and is currently in its sixth edition. Meggs authored more than a dozen other books and well over a hundred articles on graphic design and typography. He received the Association of American Publishers' Excellence in Publishing award in 1983; VCU's Award for Excellence in Teaching, Research, and Service in 1995; and the American Institute of Graphic Arts Medal posthumously in 2004. He was inducted into the Art Directors Hall of Fame in 2002.

Paul Stirton is Editor-in-Chief of *West 86th: A Journal of Decorative Arts, Design History, and Material Culture* and Professor Emeritus at Bard Graduate Center. He is the author of numerous articles and books, including *Jan Tschichold and the New Typography: Graphic Design Between the World Wars*, *Traveller's Guide to Art: Great Britain and Ireland*, and *Renaissance Painting*. He is also the coauthor of books on French art and nineteenth-century architect and design critic E. W. Godwin. He has curated exhibitions on Edward Burne-Jones and William Morris, William Blake, James McNeill Whistler, and the history of lithography.

Karen Polder is a Dutch designer who studied at the Royal Academy of Art in The Hague and the Royal College of Art (MA) in London. She designs books and exhibitions for museums and heritage institutions, including for the KB National Library of the Netherlands and for Huis van het boek, the world's oldest book museum.

Acknowledgments

Thank you to Kate Long Stellar and Paola Zanol for collections assistance; April Harper and Ellis Martin for digitization; Rickey Tax at the Huis van het boek for making collection material available for scanning; Frank Brayton for typesetting; and Kate Bolen, Stephen Coles, Ken DellaPenta, and Gail Nelson-Bonebrake for editorial assistance.

Letterform Archive
2339 Third Street, Floor 4R
San Francisco, CA 94107
letterformarchive.org

Publisher Emeritus
Rob Saunders
Publisher
Lucie Parker
Acquisitions Editor
Chris Westcott
Associate Managing Editor
Molly O'Neil Stewart
Editorial Assistant
Khoo Zi Yun (Geraldine) Ang
Art Director
Alice Chau
Print Production & Color Manager
Thomas Bollier

Design by
Karen Polder

Available through ARTBOOK | D.A.P.
75 Broad Street, Suite 630
New York, NY 10004
artbook.com

ISBN: 979-8-9891423-1-6
Library of Congress Control
Number: 2024936767

10 9 8 7 6 5 4 3 2 1
2024 2025 2026 2027 2028

Printed in China
by Artron Printing

About Letterform Archive Books

Founded in 2015 in San Francisco, Letterform Archive is a nonprofit center for design inspiration. Letterform Archive Books produces titles based on its collection of more than 100,000 artifacts spanning the history of graphic design, type design, and lettering. Its facsimile editions present rare materials from its collection in full color, preserving the experience for future readers. Historical artwork and documents may sometimes include objectionable materials, which we endeavor to address in supplemental text.

About the Artwork Reproduction

Part of Letterform Archive's mission is to preserve and share its collection in print. Collections materials are digitized in-house using state-of-the-art camera equipment and raking light, then referenced alongside proofs to ensure a perfect color match. Printed using high-resolution stochastic screening, the resulting publications feature archive-quality reproductions that faithfully re-create the experience of the originals.

About the Type

Set in Nitti Grotesk by Pieter van Rosmalen of Bold Monday. The quirky and often idiosyncratic shapes of early English sans serifs lend humanity and warmth to this multiweight sans serif family.